Improve

your Spoken English and Pronunciation

An American Accent Course for Success in Business

by Jolinda Osborne

Improve Your Spoken English and Pronunciation: American Accent for Success in Business

Audio recording of downloadable instruction by Rob Metcalf Studio
All illustrations used by permission
Covers by Barrentine Design

Published by Intercultural Communication Services, Inc., Portland, Oregon, U.S.A.
Intercultural Communication Services, Inc. publishes quality educational books and video products for non-native English speaking professionals.

ISBN: 978-1461136835

Library of Congress Catalogue Number: 2011907121

For more information about this book, to learn about other educational products, or to enquire about bulk orders, please visit *Jolinda Osborne Intercultural Communications* at **www.jolindaosborne.com**

Contents

Introduction

For over twenty years I have had the privilege of training and coaching professionals from around the world who wish to communicate effectively in English. These individuals may reside permanently or temporarily in the United States. They may be American citizens, foreign nationals working for American companies, or employees of multinational companies living in Europe, Asia, South America or Africa. They share a desire to excel in their global work environments, and they share a need to communicate well in English.

To master a spoken language – any language – involves hearing the subtlety of sound and knowing the nuance of idiom. It means becoming comfortable with new speech patterns and rhythms. It requires stretching facial muscles in very unfamiliar ways. It demands practice and long-term commitment.

Employees and students whom I've taught in classrooms or coached individually on their speech and presentation skills are committed to mastering American English pronunciation because their current jobs and future career success demand such mastery. They know they must speak up, be readily understood, be able to influence decisions, and lead others.

Improve Your Spoken English and Pronunciation: An American Accent Course for Success in Business is based on real-work experiences and a sound educational method. Individuals who use this book realize significant and noticeable improvement in their speech and pronunciation, as well as gain confidence and authority in their presentations.

This comprehensive book is complemented with seven hours of audio instruction and exercises, wherein I pronounce all the exercises in the book and give you time to practice after me and even record our voices. In the following pages you'll find instructions for downloading your free audio.

I invite you to visit my website: **www.jolindaosborne.com** to find helpful tips and other products for improving your spoken English. The **American Accent for Success in Business: A Complete Video CD-ROM Course** enables you to see me demonstrate the mouth positions for making the sounds of American English, and practice at your own pace. The **Stories for Learning Useful Business Idioms** series of short, engaging books are written for professionals like you, to help you learn the everyday vocabulary, idiomatic phrases, and American cultural references you'll need in order to understand and contribute to business conversations. From the website, please write to me with your questions and your success stories. I'd enjoy hearing from you.

Jolinda Osborne

Chapter One
Getting Started

See page 140 to download the free audio.

Clear Communication is an Essential Tool for Business Success

► **Lesson 1**

Improve your communication. You've probably received that advice from managers, mentors, friends, and even from books on career advancement. This book will help you improve your ***spoken*** communication. Whether you're conversing with coworkers, meeting a customer, presenting to senior managers, or conferencing by phone or video across an ocean, the strength of your voice and the clarity of your speech will either support or detract from your message. Clear, confident speech will compel others to listen to your ideas.

The following lessons provide a proven system for mastering American English sounds, pronunciation rules and speech patterns. You may have formally studied English or picked it up through popular culture and media. Now you will apply ***a pronunciation system*** to your own accent and speech patterns, and modify your speech so that you are always understood, have confidence, and can fully contribute your creative ideas. This book teaches ***American English***, which is fast becoming the chosen language for international business.

Verbal Communication Involves a Speaker and a Listener

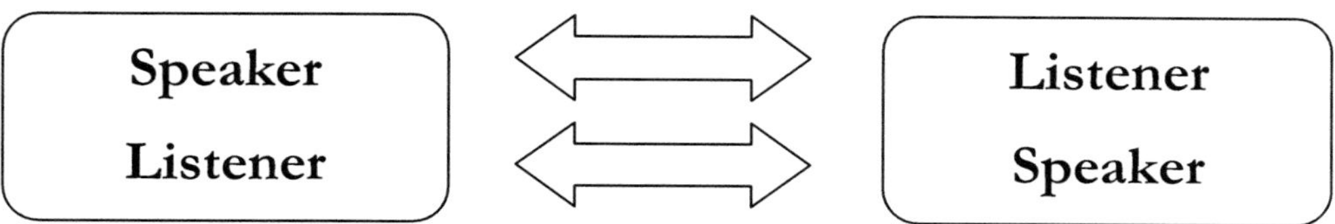

As long as the words and non-verbal signals are understood by each person, the exchange of information usually flows smoothly. Disruptions in the flow lead to misunderstanding. Reasons for disruptions include:

- ✓ An accent that is not understood
- ✓ A voice that is too soft, too low, or too high
- ✓ Lack of inflection and intonation
- ✓ Rapid speech
- ✓ Improper word or sentence stress
- ✓ Confusing non-verbal signals

Your goal is to eliminate these disruptive accent issues and speech habits so that you will be understood by everyone. This book will help you achieve this important and attainable goal. In this book you will learn:

- ✓ Which particular first-language accent issues keep other people from understanding you
- ✓ How to produce the sounds of American English
- ✓ A phonetic symbol system to train your ear, reinforce sound formation and offset problems caused by English spelling
- ✓ Pronunciation rules
- ✓ Inflection and intonation to add meaning and energy to your voice
- ✓ Breathing for pronunciation and for a strong voice
- ✓ Sentence rhythm and proper rate of speech
- ✓ How to pronounce work-related words and American idioms
- ✓ Tips for speaking on the phone
- ✓ Insight on how to minimize nervousness

Why Study Speech and Pronunciation?

After all, children learn to speak languages very easily, and without studying! Yes, from the time children first speak until about nine years of age, they are capable of learning many languages simultaneously. And they can keep them all straight in their brains!

Adult brains, however, become wired for a primary language, and the muscles of the mouth are not so flexible. Thus, most of us need to study, listen, and practice. We need to consciously "rewire" our brains and "retrain" our facial muscles.

Children learn in short spurts of intense concentration; they absorb sounds and words like a sponge. We adults have many things on our minds. Right now, in addition to reading this book, you may be thinking about a work project, what you will prepare for dinner, or how you will pay for your family holiday. All these thoughts are natural distractions.

Thus, it is important to set realistic goals for your pronunciation improvement. Completely eliminating your accent is a very difficult thing to do. It takes hours of daily effort over a long time and with a speech coach. And it's not necessary. Your accent is part of you. Many business leaders have accents. ***Instead, an achievable goal is to eliminate the accent and speech problems that keep others from understanding you, and to speak with confidence and clarity in any situation.***

Some Fundamentals of Clear Speech

Not All Sounds Produce Speech, But All Speech Requires Sound

Sound in the physical sense consists of vibrating energy moved by a force. The process of sound formation is complex, but for our purpose, the lungs take in and then force out air through the mouth or nose. Articulators such as the lips, tongue and teeth direct or block the breath stream in various ways in order to produce specific sounds.

The secret of improving your pronunciation is to understand and imitate those positions of the mouth that produce the sounds of American English. Below is a diagram of the articulators necessary to produce speech. Refer to this diagram as you proceed through the book in order to check that your tongue, lips, teeth and jaw are in the correct position for the various sounds.

Articulators and Articulation Points

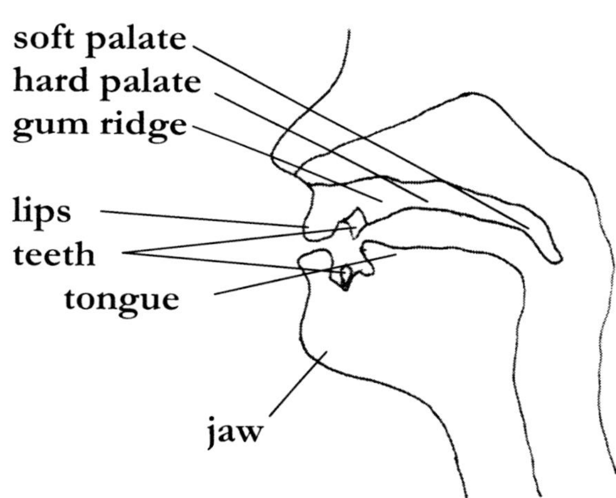

The Importance of Proper Breathing

You might think it obvious that breathing is important. Try stopping for more than a few seconds! Normally we breathe without being aware of it, but breathing for speech requires control and attention. You must quickly take in enough air to say all the words in a phrase or sentence, and then release the air gradually in order to conserve enough air to complete your sentence. Note the drawings below:

a) breathing at rest

In Out In Out

b) breathing for speech

In Out In Out

◙ Breathing Exercise: Test your lung capacity!

1) Take in a breath and say aloud the days of the week.
2) Name 20 items that you might buy at the grocery store.
3) Begin counting from *One*. How far can you go without running out of air?

If you ran out of air in a short time, you will have trouble pronouncing the consonant sounds at the end of words. Equally important, your voice will lack strength and authority.

How to Breathe Properly

There is no secret to proper breathing. All of us were born breathing correctly. Just observe a sleeping baby. The baby's abdomen moves in and out as the ***diaphragm***, the strong muscle below the chest, contracts and expands.
Refer to the diagram below.

a) The diaphragm expands [and therefore moves down] on the in-breath to allow more room for the lungs to fill with air. ***The volume of air pushes the abdomen <u>out</u> when you inhale.*** Feel your stomach move out.

b) On the out-breath, the diaphragm contracts [moves up], in order to force air from the lungs. ***The abdomen now moves <u>in</u> as you exhale.***

Note that the chest also moves in and out in response to the diaphragm, but the shoulders don't move up and down. That tight, up-down movement is the mistake most of us make in our effort to look slender. In order to get enough air for proper breathing, you must let your body respond to the movement of muscle and air.

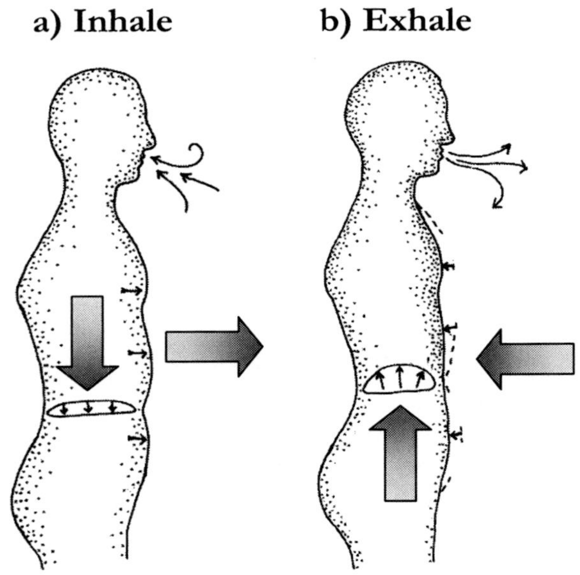

◙ Practice: Proper Breathing

1) Stand up straight. Slouching decreases lung capacity.
2) Put the palm of your hand on your abdomen [below the navel] as you breathe in. You should feel your abdomen expand. Then as you breathe out, you will feel your abdomen contract.
3) Keep your shoulders level. Stay relaxed. Breathe several times.
4) Now as you breathe properly, begin counting again from *One*.
5) Practice every day and note your improvement!

Consonants and Vowels: Important Classifications of Sounds

We categorize the sounds of American English into consonants and vowels. Depending upon your native language, you might experience more difficulty with either the consonants or the vowels. Consonants and vowel sounds are challenging in different ways.

Consonants are formed when the flow of air is interrupted or diverted by the teeth, tongue, lips or soft palate. Proper pronunciation of consonants requires a very active mouth, and you will need to move the facial muscles in new and uncomfortable ways.

Consonants are distinguished as either voiced or voiceless. Voiced consonants are produced with vibration of the vocal cords. Voiceless consonants are produced with the breath alone. This is an important concept that you will encounter throughout the book.

Vowels are formed when the breath stream is not interrupted but is altered by the lips, teeth or tongue. Thus, proper pronunciation of vowels requires that you listen carefully to the subtle differences in sounds and notice the slight shifts in the position of your tongue and lips. ***All vowels are voiced.***

◙ Practice: Making Voiced and Voiceless Sounds

Place your fingers lightly around your throat and say the words **bay** and **pay**. You should feel vibration when you say [b]. It's a ***voiced*** consonant. The [p] is ***voiceless*** and is made only with the breath. There is no vibration. The [b] and [p] are distinguished by their voicing, but they are otherwise produced in the same way.

The voiced consonant is often harder to produce than the unvoiced one, particularly when the voiced sound comes at the end of a word. The [b] in **bat** may be fairly easy to say, but many non-native speakers find the [b] in **tab** to be much harder. Often, the [b] at the end of **tab** is mispronounced [p], as in **tap**, or else it's simply not said at all, leaving the listener to wonder what *ta* means!

Stress and Intonation: Keys to Speaking Like an American

English is a stressed language. ***Stress*** is the emphasis given to a particular syllable within a word, or to a particular word within a group of words or a sentence. ***Accent*** is another term that also refers to the stress within an individual word. The accent or stress mark [´] is used to indicate the stress point[s] in a word or sentence.

Make every effort to get into the habit of marking in your book the stressed syllable in unfamiliar words. Mis-stressing words is a common mistake that causes others to misunderstand you; for example, the word **maintenance** is pronounced **máin te nance**, (not **main té nance**).

Listen closely to native speakers; they will almost always stress the word correctly. Your dictionary is a good resource for determining stress.

Stress has an important role in giving American English, or any other language, its particular rhythm. To the extent that you master stress, you will develop a more fluid, easily understood manner of speaking.

Intonation is the melody of a language. Intonation occurs as the voice rises or falls to form rhythmic patterns that are recognizably American. By changing the intonation you can change the emphasis or even the meaning of your message. When the voice glides up or down while saying a single word, we call that movement ***inflection***. Both intonation and inflection give speech its vitality and emotional meaning.

You will have an opportunity in each chapter to practice raising and lowering your voice in order to add emphasis and interest to your speech. If your voice lacks intonation, you will speak in a flat, monotone manner, and others will be bored by what you say, and may quit listening.

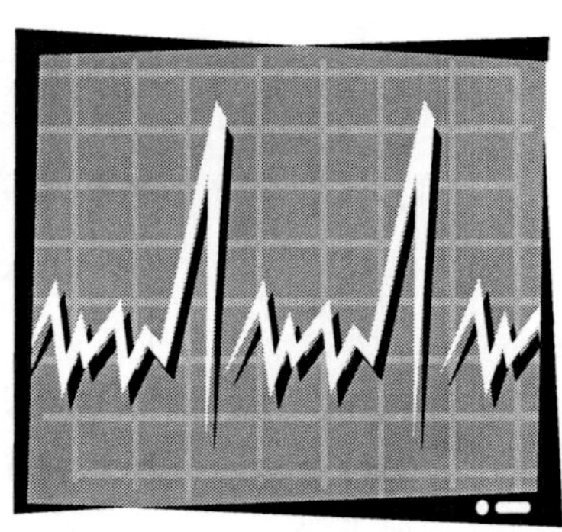

The International Phonetic Alphabet [IPA]: A Tool for Improving Your Pronunciation

The IPA is a set of phonetic symbols developed about a hundred years ago to help people pronounce words. Each symbol represents one sound. Thus, when you hear an unfamiliar word, you can capture its correct pronunciation by writing down the symbols. Or, if you see a symbol, you will know exactly the sound that it represents.

It is important to distinguish ***sound*** from ***letters.*** English spelling is confusing. For example: the letters ***oo*** are pronounced differently in these four words: **moon** [u] **look** [ʊ] **blood** [ʌ] and **brooch** [o]. It's enough to make you despair of ever mastering the language. However, the IPA symbols identify which sound the letters ***oo*** represent.

Another advantage of adding the IPA to your communication toolbox is that you will become a better listener. Keen listening is essential to correct pronunciation. Once you can distinguish sounds, you will consciously be able to position your mouth to produce the correct sound of each syllable in a word.

We have 26 letters in English, but 40+ sounds [depending on how one categorizes American dialects]. On pages 148 to 149 you will find a list of the IPA symbols that will be covered in this book on American English. The list is a handy reference, but don't feel you must memorize the symbols. They will become familiar as you work with the words and exercises in each chapter.

How to Get the Most out of this Course

1) **Familiarize yourself with the organization of the chapters.** Each chapter contains exercises that will help you speak more clearly, and will introduce you to vocabulary and phrases often heard in the workplace.
   - ✓ **Instructions** on how to produce the key sounds
   - ✓ **Contrast Pairs** that contrast the key sounds with other similar sounds
   - ✓ **Words at Work** that contain the key sounds
   - ✓ **Practice Sentences** that emphasize the sounds and provide you with opportunities to improve your intonation and inflection
   - ✓ **Phrases and Idioms** for practicing rhythm and intonation
   - ✓ **Work-related Dialogues** focused on the key sounds
   - ✓ **Pronunciation Rules and Tips** for more effective speech at work

2) **Listen to the exercises in each lesson.** Once you have downloaded the audio that accompanies the course, listen each day to Jolinda as she reads words, phrases and sentences.

3) **Practice the exercises aloud.** Jolinda will pause after words, phrases and sentences, and sometimes within sentences, so that you can repeat them. You may want to record yourself and Jolinda, play back, and notice how closely you come to Jolinda's pronunciation.

4) **Keep the audio with you in your car or in your player.** Just a few minutes of practice each day will make a noticeable difference in your ability to speak American English more fluidly.

5) **Determine your learning strategy for improving your pronunciation.**
   - ✓ You may wish to go through the book from beginning to end. The sounds are arranged according to how the position of the mouth changes.
   - ✓ If you are a more advanced speaker, or if you have had previous pronunciation training, refer to the Contents to find the sounds/lessons that you know are problematic for you.
   - ✓ Refer to the Troublesome Sounds by First Language beginning on page 150 to be guided to those sounds/lessons most important for you to study.

6) **Practice. Practice. Practice!**
   - ✓ Focus 15 minutes a day on your English pronunciation.
   - ✓ Listen to English on the radio, TV, at the movies. Imitate the speakers.

7) **Pay attention to the pronunciation of foreign words.** Foreign names and proper nouns used in the book are given an American pronunciation and stress. If you encounter a word from your country of origin that you pronounce differently, you are indeed entitled to think, "We don't say it that way." However, since your focus is to learn a pronunciation system that Americans find familiar and that is useful in the international business environment, knowledge of American pronunciation is beneficial.

8) **Expand your professional vocabulary.** An important way to improve your communication is to expand your spoken vocabulary. At work you may avoid saying the precise word that expresses your meaning because you're unsure of its pronunciation. Mispronunciations can be embarrassing. Unfortunately, you end up limiting your ideas because you have limited your spoken vocabulary. Therefore, pay attention to how words are pronounced in the book and on the audio.

9) Learn idiomatic expressions. American English, like many languages, is full of expressions and phrases that may be confusing to you. Americans interject these idioms during their meetings at work, and in their everyday conversations. A few idioms or expressions are provided in each lesson as another way to practice the sounds highlighted in that lesson.

10) Make English pronunciation a priority in your life by committing to the following daily activities:

◙ **Daily Activity #1:** Write down words, phrases or idiomatic expressions that you encounter at work. Perhaps you've mispronounced the word or hesitated to use it for fear of being incorrect.

Bring those words or phrases to a teacher, coach, coworker, mentor or friend. Ask for help with pronunciation or syllable stress. Use an online dictionary that will pronounce the word for you.

Then take the words back into your work environment and use your expanded spoken vocabulary with confidence.

◙ **Daily Activity #2:** Become aware of and write down as best you can the words and phrases you use that others seem not to understand. You'll know if they ask you to repeat, or give you a blank stare.

Check the pronunciation and syllable stress with a colleague or friend, or listen to the pronunciation with an online dictionary.

Now, it's time to begin improving your American English.
Good luck as you study the lessons!

It does not matter how slowly you go as long as you do not stop.
~ Confucius

Chapter Two
The "Plosives"

[p, b, t, d, k, g]

Plosives are sounds that you make by blocking the breath stream for a short time, but long enough to build up air pressure behind your teeth and lips. Then you suddenly "explode" this air to produce a sound.

[p - b]

► **Lesson 2**

Place of Articulation: lips

Classification: [p] voiceless
[b] voiced

Sentences: [p] The part-time employee received praise for her help on the project in Spain.

[b] Bob and Barbara basked in the sun in Bermuda on their sabbaticals from work.

Production: To say [p], press your lips together firmly and keep your teeth slightly apart. Build up air pressure in your mouth, and don't let any air escape through your nose. Then let the air force your lips apart with an audible explosion. You should feel a puff of air if you hold your palm to your mouth.

To say [b], press your lips a little more firmly together. Start to voice sound while your lips are still together. You should not feel any puff of air as your lips part.

Be Aware of these Problems with [p] and [b]

Some speakers [Asians, Indians, Arabs, various Pacific Islanders] substitute [b] when trying to say [p]. The key to saying [p] is to lightly close your lips.

- It is especially hard for many non-native speakers to voice [b] at the end of a word.
  - **Correction**: Reserve enough air to make the ending sound.
- [b] and [v] are often spoken interchangeably by Spanish speakers.
  - **Correction**: Lots of practice. The lips close for [b], while the upper teeth are on the lower lip for [v]. Look at your mouth in the mirror while you contrast the sounds.

Contrast Pairs:

[p]	[b]	[p]	[b]
pet	bet	mop	mob
pond	bond	pole	bowl
cap	cab	pen	Ben
rope	robe	pear	bear
pie	buy	rip	rib
nip	nib	cup	cub
sip	sib	pull	bull
pay	bay	nap	nab
gap	gab	Pete	beet
peep	beep	putt	but
pin	bin	pack	back
pat	bat	pup	pub

Words at Work:

Beginning	*Middle*	*End*
password	happen	tape
bargain	enable	globe
plant	unpaid	grasp
brochure	rubbed	scrub
person	appear	chip
background	combine	web
plastic	appropriate	strip
burst	tabulate	stub
process	repair	prep
balanced	October	disturb
prize	approve	scrap
billion	website	tube

Practice Sentences for [p] and [b]

1. The personnel department produced a brochure on benefits.
2. I prefer a big breakfast before beginning my day.
3. Please input the numbers into the database on my computer.
4. He bruised his ribs when he bumped into the building.
5. It's better to buy a few expensive gifts than many cheap ones.
6. The President appeared behind the podium.
7. Special procedures apply when dealing with big batches.
8. The police nabbed the robbers before their bomb exploded.
9. There may be special taxes on imported products.
10. Employees were paid a bonus in December.
11. The proprietor in the bazaar bartered for pencils.

Troublesome Blends:

[pl]	[pr]	[bl]	[br]
apply	pressure	block	breakfast
plant	practice	assemble	broadcast
plaque	project	stable	brainstorm
ample	produce	blip	breathe
explicit	prepare	blend	brand
hopeless	praise	blast	break

Note other troublesome words with these blends.

_______	_______	_______	_______
_______	_______	_______	_______
_______	_______	_______	_______

♫ **Intonation:** Repeat these phrases, some of which are American idioms. Emphasize the accented syllable to add rhythm and interest to your voice.

personnél department	burst búbble	employee pénsion
the best bét	a global présence	bread and bútter
Play báll!	a bad hábit	Arabian Península
a pair of pánts	bánking business	a billion býtes

♫ **Intonation:** Practice raising your voice at the end of a question sentence when you expect a "yes" or "no" answer.

Example: Are you feeling better? ↗
Yes. ↘

1. Did you pay off your debt to the bank?
2. Does this black umbrella belong to you?
3. Will my presentation be taped?
4. Should we scrap the bad components?
5. Will the plant produce the parts on time?
6. Is our PR department publishing the report?
7. Have you proofread the white paper?
8. Can I practice my pronunciation with you?
9. Were the robbers captured?
10. Will the boxes of bananas be shipped today?
11. Do you prefer birds as pets?
12. Must we assemble each part before the inspection?

 **Words with the letter p where the consonant is silent.**

receipt
corps

 **Words with the letter b where the consonant is silent.**

debt
bomb
comb
subtle

[t – d]

► **Lesson 3**

Place of Articulation: tongue tip and upper gum ridge

Classification: [t] voiceless
[d] voiced

Sentences: [t] Tan tossed two extra tires into his truck.

[d] Then he closed the back and drove down the road.

Production: To say [t], touch the tip of your tongue to the gum ridge behind your upper front teeth. Be careful not to touch the tongue tip to your teeth. Use air pressure to force your tongue away sharply, so that air escapes from between the teeth.

To say [d], follow the directions for [t], but as air pressure begins to force your tongue away from the gum ridge, add voice.

Be Aware of these Problems with [t] and [d]

- [d] is often substituted for [t] in the middle of words. Ex: *budder* instead of **butter**.
    - **Correction**: Enunciate the sounds. Slow down.
- Asian and many other language speakers often fail to pronounce the final voiced consonant: Thus, they might say *rai* instead of **raid**.
    - **Correction**: Save enough air to make the final [d] sound.
- Many speakers confuse [t] and [d] in the final position.
    - **Correction**: Enunciate and slow down. [d] is usually harder to say.
- Speakers of Spanish and other Latin-based languages may put their tongue against the back of the front teeth instead of on the gum ridge, thus producing an unclear sound.
    - **Correction**: Don't touch your tongue tip to your upper teeth.

Contrast Pairs:

[t]	[d]	[t]	[d]	[t]	[d]
tin	din	train	drain	tense	dense
bitter	bidder	latter	ladder	heat	heed
bright	bride	moat	mode	feet	feed
bat	bad	hat	had	catty	caddy
tide	died	neater	kneader	try	dry
time	dime	kitty	kiddy	knot	nod
tuck	duck	otter	odder	coat	code
title	tidal	rated	raided	beat	bead
tore	door	debt	dead	tear	dare
toe	doe	tomb	doom	sat	sad
team	deem	true	drew	neat	need
tangle	dangle	utter	udder	brat	brad

 **Words with the letter t where the consonant is silent.**

often listen whistle fasten

Other words you encounter with silent **t**:

______ ______ ______ ______

Words at Work:

Beginning	*Middle*	*End*
template	attribute	invest
daily	leader	board
test site	Internet	instruct
dispute	indicator	beyond
twenty	contributor	offset
data	advertise	proceed
Tuesday	output	jet
detail	outdated	weld
Tokyo	enterprise	forest
drive	solder	standard
tonnage	between	noticed
drastic	adjust	brand

Rule for Pronunciation of the Final Letters ***ed***

Many non-native speakers become confused by the pronunciation of the ***ed*** ending of regular verbs. Here is a rule that will help you.

- If the sound preceding ***ed*** is voiceless, pronounce the ***ed*** as [t]. Examples:
  raced = [rest] locked = [lakt] washed = [waʃt] laughed = [læft]

- If the sound preceding ***ed*** is voiced, pronounce the ***ed*** as [d]. Examples:
  lived = [lɪvd] named = [nemd] pleased = [plizd] edged = [ɛdʒd]

- If the sound preceding ***ed*** is a [d] or a [t], the ***ed*** is pronounced as a separate syllable. Examples:
  estimated = [ɛstɪmetəd] provided = [provaɪdɛd]
  *This final syllable can be pronounced [ɛd] or [əd].

This rule works! Remember that spoken language [any language] evolved much earlier than written language, so people spoke in a manner that flowed naturally: voiced to voiced, voiceless to voiceless. Rules came much later.

Note: Vowels are voiced, so the ending sound is [d]. Example: tried = [traɪd]

◙ **Exercise: Write the correct ending sound symbols beside the word.**

pushed ____	developed _____	instructed _____
learned ____	wedged _____	coughed _____
picked ____	dialed _____	emailed _____
wanted ____	stopped _____	attended _____

Practice Sentences for [t] and [d]

1. The advertisement for temporary help produced results.
2. A dozen defective parts were returned.
3. A heater is standard equipment for trucks in cold climates.
4. David should have deleted the angry words in his letter.
5. Please route the report to all departments.
6. The western coast of Ireland encounters many storms.
7. Our worldwide customers ordered lots of new products.
8. The sports industry is dependent upon TV and cable media.
9. The past is behind us; the future is ahead. So live in the present moment.
10. The metal rusted, so it had to be replaced.
11. Our factory adopted best management practices.
12. During the weekend, we toured an historic battle site.

A Pronunciation Tip

The sound [t] followed by an [n] or [l] in words such as **little, mountain,** or **metal** can be a difficult combination of sounds for many non-native speakers to produce. It's not hard, though. Here's the trick: ***Don't let your tongue move away from the gum ridge after making the [t].*** Thus, in the word **little**, touch your tongue tip to the gum ridge and then hold the tongue tip there while the sides drop, to explode the air laterally. When saying the word **certain**, keep the tongue tip on the gum ridge, drop the soft palate, and let the air come out the nose.

Practice words

total	petal	battle	metal
settle	bottle	bitten	cotton
certain	button	mountain	rotten

Troublesome Blends: [tr] [dr]

After producing the [t] or [d] sound, move your tongue off the gum ridge and then roll it back to say [r]. ***Don't slide your tongue along the palate.*** Try this exercise. Start slowly. Gradually shorten the pause between phonemes.

Tuh…ree	tuh..ree	tuh.ree	tuhree	tree
Duh…rive	duh..rive	duh.rive	duhrive	drive

◙ **Practice the following words**:

train	travel	translate	trip	attract	trial
drain	address	hundred	drag	draft	drive

♫ **Intonation:** Repeat these phrases, some of which are American idioms. Emphasize the accented syllable to add rhythm and interest to your voice.

trick or tréat	deleted dáta	wórldwide distribútion
daily dose of médicine	wáste not wánt not	the middle gróund
little by líttle	wórked like a dóg	burned the midnight óil
the tráin station	the burly bódyguard	collected the dáta

▣ **Idea for a Conversation:** Recall a memorable trip you once took. Perhaps you traveled by train, rode the bus, or drove your car. Talk to a friend or colleague about the highlights of the trip. Remember to speak in the past tense.

The need to communicate effectively with your customers will come up again and again.
~ Bill Gates

[k – g]

► **Lesson 4**

Place of Articulation: back of tongue and soft palate

Classification: [k] voiceless
[g] voiced

Sentences: [k] The clerk used his key to lock up the school equipment once the science experiment was completed.

[g] Gary examined the schedule and realized that he needed to spend more time guiding his project group.

Production: To say [k], open your mouth slightly and touch the back of your tongue against the soft palate. Build up air pressure behind the tongue. Quickly release the tongue, making a noticeable explosion.

To say [g], produce voice as the tongue begins to block the stream of air.

Be Aware of these Problems with [k] and [g]

- Many non-native speakers interchange the [g] and [k]. This is a problem of voicing. It's not difficult to correct. Just remember that [k] is voiceless, and there is no vibration in your throat as you produce it. When you make [g], however, you produce a small grunt.
- Many speakers omit the [k] sound in words spelled with ***cc*** or ***ex***. The following words all have the [k] sound followed by [s].

accept	accident	excite	extra
exposure	accessory	success	except
experiential	excerpt	excavate	experiment

Contrast Pairs:

[k]	[g]	[k]	[g]	[k]	[g]
coal	goal	ankle	angle	ache	egg
cane	gain	sacking	sagging	luck	lug
crow	grow	clocking	clogging	snack	snag
core	gore	picky	piggy	leak	league
craze	graze	mucky	muggy	hack	hag
crab	grab	bicker	bigger	tack	tag
card	guard	decree	degree	stack	stag
cold	gold	re-cane	regain	buck	bug
coast	ghost	plucking	plugging	hock	hog
curl	girl	hackle	haggle	knack	nag
cash	gash	backing	bagging	wick	wig
came	game	snicker	snigger	slack	slag

Rule for the Pronunciation of the Letter *x*

These simple rules will help you distinguish between words with the letter ***x*** that are pronounced [gz] and those that are pronounced [ks].

- If the <u>vowel</u> sound following the **x** is stressed, the **x** is pronounced [gz].
  Example: ex<u>a</u>ctly, example, exhibit, exempt, exist, exuberant, exact
- When *x* is followed by a ***pronounced consonant*** or an ***unstressed vowel***, it is pronounced [ks].
  Example: ex<u>i</u>t, extra, execute, explain, excuse, experiment
- Words that end in **x** are pronounced with a [ks]. Example: fax, box, fix

Words at Work:

Beginning	*Middle*	*End*
chemistry	architect	backpack
graphic	goggles	colleague
case	increase	strike
group	regulate	analog
customer	inquire	Bangkok
gross	rigorous	flag
gasket	fragment	dialogue
continent	accomplish	peak
gauge	anger	league
cashier	perfect	mistake
ground	organize	log
criteria	practical	spec

Practice Sentences for [k] and [g]

1. Carlo created the graphics for our new logo.
2. We're all looking for the goose that lays exotic golden eggs.
3. We expect exact figures on defects that come from the factory.
4. Kim created chaos when he mixed chemicals in the school lab.
5. Kids are welcome at the company picnic.
6. The captain navigated his oil tanker across the Pacific.
7. A worker at the construction site flagged down our vehicle.
8. The Oregon high-technology area is called Silicon Forest.
9. The architect for our corporate headquarters is great.
10. We never compromise on quality for our customers.
11. Gilbert got a signature to buy protective glasses for the crew.
12. Let's focus on our successes, not on our mistakes.

Difficult Blends:

[kl]	[kr]	[kt]	[kw]
client	crew	active	quiet
claim	recruit	product	request
cycle	create	impact	qualify
clean	decrease	practice	inquire
incline	screen	duct	question
circle	credit	trucked	equipment

Difficult Blends:

[gl]	[gr]	[gz]	[gd]
glass	grew	example	logged
global	regret	exhaust	flagged
neglect	grateful	bugs	lugged
angle	grease	zigzags	tugged
glove	agree	jogs	fatigued
legal	gram	exempt	rigged

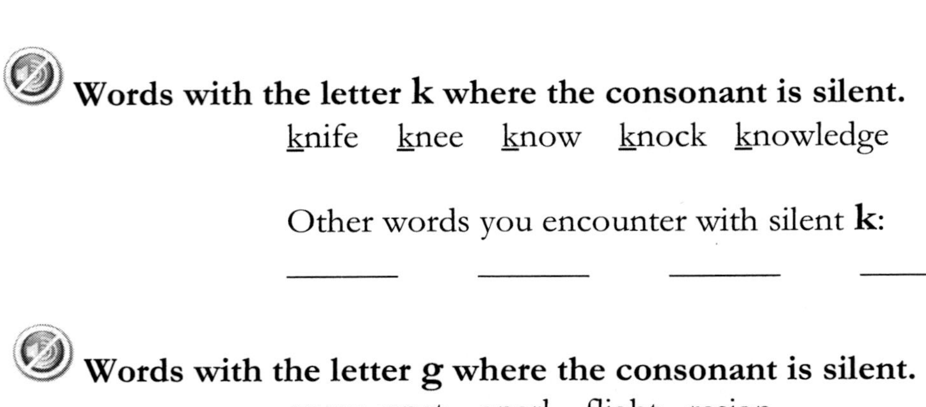

Words with the letter k where the consonant is silent.

knife knee know knock knowledge

Other words you encounter with silent **k**:

_______ _______ _______ ______

Words with the letter g where the consonant is silent.

gnaw gnat gnarl flight resign

Other words you encounter with silent **g**

_______ _______ _______ ______

♫ **Intonation:** Repeat these phrases, some of which are American idioms. Emphasize the accented syllable to add rhythm and interest to your voice.

the gift of gáb	a competent créw	cóffee with créam
fít for a kíng	Gírl Scouts	all his éggs in one básket
a clove of gárlic	the Alaska góld rush	Olympic góld
Grand Cányon	an escápe clause	íncome tax

Review of the Plosives: [p] [b] [t] [d] [k] [g]

§ Tongue Twisters: Take a moment to study the sentences. Then read them aloud, making sure you sound all the consonants.

1. Bank robbers always buy crab cakes before breaking in to buildings.
2. Ducks quack, quails wail, larks hark, but my cat barks.
3. A tarantula accidentally tripped over Todd's toes and let out a grunt.
4. The angler in Uganda grabbed a gaff and bagged his catch.
5. The burly bear brought her cub to the boat and begged for a pineapple.
6. Tourists traveling through Turkey taste dozens of tantalizing treats.
7. The demented dentist handed out bags of candy to all the kids.
8. A dog doesn't bite the hand that feeds him if the food comes daily.
9. A paper plate placed beside Pierre had pears, pecans, and ketchup.
10. The crew guided the canoe across a lake clogged with crocodiles.
11. Glassblowers gather the goods from the glory hole, and then blow.
12. Peter Piper picked a pail of pink pickled peppers.

Word Wise: List troublesome words you encounter at work or elsewhere. Perhaps you've mispronounced the word, or hesitated to use it and thus limited your ability to express yourself. Add the phonetic symbols, or ask for help in sounding out the word.

____________	____________	____________	____________
____________	____________	____________	____________
____________	____________	____________	____________
____________	____________	____________	____________
____________	____________	____________	____________
____________	____________	____________	____________
____________	____________	____________	____________
____________	____________	____________	____________

►◄ **Dialogue**: Have fun with the following dialogue. In addition to focusing on the English sounds covered in this chapter, remember to use intonation and stress in order to give your voice more life and your words more expression. The dialogue contains American idioms and informal speech patterns.

Cubicle Conversation

Todd: What's up? You look pleased.

Prakesh: My presentation was a big hit.

Todd: Great! So the project was funded?

Prakesh: Yep. And a technician from DTB has been added to my team.

Todd: I trust Binh and Pat are giving you support.

Prakesh: Pat brought me up to speed on the calibration process.

Todd: Pat's the best. She knows calibration like the back of her hand.

Prakesh: And Binh is already supplying me with test results.

Todd: Great! Next you'll be presenting your idea to upper management.

Prakesh: Don't you think I should wait until Q2?

Todd: You're probably right. Better get some robust test results first.

Prakesh: Our team is going to dig right in and examine the data from DTB.

Todd: Okay. Oops! I'm scheduled for another meeting. Let's pick up the discussion later.

Chapter Three
The "Streamers, Sizzlers and Buzzers"
[Fricatives]

[f] [v] [θ] [ð] [s] [z] [ʃ] [ʒ] [h]

**The fricatives sounds are formed,
not by blocking the breath stream completely,
but by narrowly opening the mouth
just enough to allow air to escape.**

[f – v]

► **Lesson 5**

Place of Articulation: lower lip and upper teeth

Classification: [f] voiceless
[v] voiced

Sentences: [f] Half the group laughed while doing physical exercise.

[v] A savvy traveler is very fond of cheap airfares.

Production: To produce [f], lightly touch the cutting edge of your upper front teeth to your lower lip. Rest your tongue along the bottom of your mouth, behind the teeth. Start the breath moving between your lower lip and upper teeth.

To produce [v] add voice as you feel your teeth and lips touch.

Be Aware of these Problems with [f] and [v]

- Many Asian and Arab language speakers fail to produce [v] at the end of words, or they substitute the voiceless [f].
    - **Correction**: Save enough air to make the voiced [v].
- German speakers, and others, may confuse [f] and [v].
    - **Correction**: Concentrate on producing the proper sound.
- Speakers of Hindi, Tamil and Urdu often substitute [w] for [v].
    - **Correction**: Watch yourself in a mirror as you say [v]. You must place your teeth on your lower lip. Don't round your lips at all.
- Spanish speakers may substitute [b] for [v].
    - **Correction**: Watch yourself in a mirror as you produce each sound. You must touch your teeth to your lower lip for [v]. Your lips are closed for [b]. The sounds may be interchanged in Spanish, but they are very different in English.

Contrast Pairs

[f]	[v]	[f]	[v]	[b]	[v]	[w]	[v]
fail	veil	raffle	ravel	bat	vat	went	vent
focal	vocal	final	vinyl	ban	van	wine	vine
fender	vendor	ferry	very	saber	saver	west	vest
infest	invest	fee	V	best	vest	wail	veil
wafer	waver	half	halve	boat	vote	worse	verse
proof	prove	fault	vault	bail	vale	wend	vend
safe	save	few	view	bend	vend	wow	vow
belief	believe	feud	viewed	bane	vane	wane	vain
feel	veal	leaf	leave	base	vase	grew	groove
fan	van	fast	vast	bow	vow	wet	vet
face	vase	shuffle	shovel	beer	veer	wiper	viper
fine	vine	surface	service	dub	dove	wile	vile

Words at Work:

platform
visual
foreign
valve
fifty
evolve
graph
advocate
tough
verbal
Philippines
division

configure
server
affordable
device
default
observe
fix
versatile
hand off
verify
professional
survey

photography
advertise
rephrase
invisible
perform
various
phase
previous
inflation
evaluate
tariff
productive

Practice Sentences for [f] and [v]

1. The very first harvest of grapes makes the finest wine.
2. The shelves held many types of valves and other devices.
3. A foreign vessel carrying food arrived at the waterfront.
4. Our vendors supply us with a variety of vitamins.
5. We should invest in infrastructure for our future.
6. Frequent fliers view the world from above.
7. Our firm's values drive our performance.
8. Victor served me a large dish of vanilla ice cream.
9. Defects in the factory affect the bottom line.
10. Fred gave us a brief overview of how to grow coffee.
11. Phillip failed to tell the staff about his family fortune.

Rule for the Preposition *of*

The preposition ***of*** contains the voiced sound [v] and is pronounced [ʌv]. Say the following phrases, making sure to voice [v]. The sound is not strong, but it's there.

bag of tricks	cup of coffee	bowl of soup
pair of pants	field of flowers	one of the jobs
day of rest	lots of money	glass of water
book of poems	festival of music	end of the road

Difficult Blends

[fl]	[fr]	[vl]	[vz]
flame	France	gravel	shaves
deflect	freeze	survival	moves
floor	Africa	travel	halves
flex	refresh	rival	curves
flash	front	level	resolves
flatten	friction	bevel	grooves
scuffle	fresh	gavel	serves
waffle	Francisco	oval	preserves
influence	fruit	shovel	proves
float	fracture	swivel	fives
flour	frail	anvil	wolves
fluctuate	friend	novel	strives

Inflection

Inflection is the movement [higher or lower] within a word as you produce voice. Rising inflection can signal a yes/no question, or it might invite the listener to be attentive to what you will say next. Falling inflection signals the end of a thought, certainty, or emphasis.

Example: If I make more money, I'll purchase a plane ticket.

In this example, the "If…" clause is incomplete without the rest of the sentence. By gliding your voice upward with the word **money**, you create expectation and interest. Your listener will wait for you to finish your thought.

◙ **Practice: Add inflection to the following sentences.**

1. If we go to the market, I'll buy flowers for our visitors.
2. If Frederick finds his book, he'll read a few chapters tonight.
3. If the sun doesn't rise tomorrow, we'll all be very worried.
4. If I played the flute, I'd entertain the Queen.
5. If French fries weren't so fatty, I'd eat them for breakfast.
6. If fish had wings, few of us would ever catch one for dinner.
7. If my fingers weren't so stiff, I'd carry the dishes.
8. If feathers were heavy, birds couldn't fly.
9. If you add vinegar, you'll spoil the soup.
10. If the river floods, the villagers will flee to higher ground.
11. If I were fifteen again, I'd follow my heart.
12. If my daughter has a child, she'll name the child after me.

▣ **Idea for a Conversation**: Have you ever speculated about what you would do if you were to win the lottery? Tell a friend or colleague how your life might change. Begin your conversation this way: "If I won the lottery, I would….."

[θ - ð]

▶ **Lesson 6**

Place of Articulation: tongue tip between teeth

Classification: [θ] voiceless
[ð] voiced

Sentences: [θ] Thanks for the thick bath towels.

[ð] The weather forecast predicts a southern breeze.

Production: To produce [θ], open your mouth and slightly part your teeth. Round the tip of your tongue and place it ***between*** your upper and lower teeth. Your tongue should protrude slightly. Force air between your tongue and teeth, and keep your tongue out while you expel air.

To produce the voiced [ð], begin adding vibration as soon as your tongue touches your teeth.

Be Aware of these Problems with [θ] and [ð]

- These are very difficult sounds for most non-native speakers to master. The sounds do not exist in most other languages, and even American children find them hard; they are two of the last sounds children acquire.
- Problems with the voiceless [θ]
  - Many people substitute a [t] = ***tin*** instead of **thin**
  - Others substitute [s] = ***sin*** instead of **thin**
- Problems with the voiced [ð]
  - Many people substitute [d] = ***dem*** instead of **them**
  - Others substitute [z] = ***zem*** instead of **them**

- The ***key to correct pronunciation is to protrude your tongue slightly between your teeth.*** You cannot make the sounds if you keep your tongue hidden inside your mouth!
- Practice in front of a mirror so that you can see your tongue. This new position will feel strange at first. That's okay. It means you're probably doing it correctly.

Contrast Pairs:

[θ]	[t]	[θ]	[s] or [ʃ]
thin	tin	thank	sank
thick	tick	thing	sing
theme	team	thread	shred [ʃ]
thong	tong	thumb	some
math	mat	math	mass
both	boat	mouth	mouse
booth	boot	path	pass
Beth	bet	bath	bass
oaths	oats	wealth	Welsh [ʃ]
death	debt	with	wish [ʃ]
forth	fort	unthinkable	unsinkable
ether	eater	thigh	sigh

Contrast Pairs:

[ð]	[d]	[ð]	[z]
though	dough	then	Zen
those	doze	bathe	bays
they	day	breathed	breezed
their	dare	clothe	close
lather	ladder	loathe	lows
breathe	breed	tithe	ties
worthy	wordy	soothe	sues
than	Dan	teethe	tease
other	udder	lathe	laze
seethe	seed	writhe	rise
then	den	sheathe	she's
seething	seeding	clothed	closed

Words at Work:	*Beginning*	*Middle*	*End*
[θ]	thorough	method	beneath
	thousand	ethnic	wealth
	thumb	withhold	growth
	thread	truthful	south
	third	everything	north
	thought	anthem	bandwidth
[ð]	therefore	leather	bathe
	though	whether	soothe
	those	brother	breathe
	thereafter	another	seethe
	thus	farther	worthy

Practice Sentences for [θ] and [ð]

1. On Thursday three employees met in the north conference room.
2. Physical therapy can be helpful for athletic injuries.
3. Thelma enjoys the weather in the Netherlands.
4. The Northern Lights bathe the night sky with color.
5. I'll buy my mother a leather bag or feather jacket for her birthday.
6. Jose's third floor office has a southern exposure.
7. The theory relied on a mathematical formula.
8. The smooth machine parts were bathed in a chemical solution.
9. Three teeth in my mouth were pulled before Mother's Day.
10. Proper breathing is important before a big speech.
11. Athens is both an ancient and modern city.
12. Father is a worthy tradesman. He makes excellent pottery on the lathe.

Rule: When to Say [θ] or [ð] with the Spelling *th*

Speakers are often confused about how to pronounce a word with the letters ***th***. Here is a rule to help you determine the pronunciation.

- Say the voiceless [θ] when the ***th*** follows a pronounced consonant.
  Example: mo<u>n</u>th, <u>m</u>ath, <u>s</u>outh, a<u>n</u>ything
- Say the voiced [ð] when the word ends in ***ther***. Example: mother, weather
- Say the voiced [ð] when the word ends in ***the***. Examples: soothe, breathe, lathe
  Note that the word *smooth* [smuð] is an exception.

Ordinal Numbers

Ordinal numbers, so called because they indicate the order of something, [fourth, hundredth] are commonly used at work, and they are particularly difficult to pronounce. Unfortunately, there's no easy method for proper pronunciation. Slow down so that your tongue has time to make each sound and move to the following sound. However, don't stop between sounds. Remember to stick your tongue out between your teeth and keep your breath stream flowing as you produce the voiceless [θ] at the end of the numbers.

fourth	hundredth
fifth	thousandth
sixth	
seventh	
eighth	
ninth	
tenth	

Keep going: eleventh…...twelfth……thirteenth…..

☺Now add [s] at the end of the words for an *additional* challenge: fourths, fifths, sixths, hundredths…..

◙ **Practice:** Write down the numbers you use most often at work. Take time to practice them.

__________ __________ __________ __________ __________

Pronunciation Rule for the Word *the*

- The definite article ***the*** is pronounced with the unstressed vowel [ə] when it's followed by a word beginning with a consonant. Examples: the stockroom, the manager, the report
- ***The*** is pronounced with the vowel [ɪ] when it is followed by a word beginning with a vowel. Examples: the application, the effort, the opening
- You may choose to say the vowel [i] anytime you want to stress the definite article. Examples: This is ***the*** [ði] best restaurant in town!

♫ **Intonation:** Repeat the following phrases, some of which are American idioms. Emphasize the accented syllable to add rhythm and interest to your voice.

nothing but the trúth	the wéather report	through thíck and thín
the grándfather clause	the mouth of the ríver	the lovely leather jácket
the seaworthy shíp	the fourth estáte	the thoughtful yóuths
the clóthing store	the three ténors	the athlétic shoes

▣ **Ideas for a Conversation**

- Your ideal weather, and how you would enjoy that weather
- A destination either north or south of your home, where you would enjoy a day outing or a short vacation
- Something in your life that you are thankful for

[s - z]

► **Lesson 7**

Place of Articulation: tip and sides of the tongue

Classification: [s] voiceless
[z] voiced

Sentences: [s] In Paris you find the scent of perfume even in the grass.
[z] Please prune the Zen Garden roses.

Production: To produce [s], place the tip of your tongue in the position to say [t], but don't say it. Then drop the tongue tip down and pull it back slightly. Press the sides of the tongue against the inside upper teeth. The tip should be pointing at the cutting edge of your front teeth. Make a hissing, voiceless sound.
To produce [z], add voice as the air begins to move.

Be Aware of these Problems with [s] and [z]

Most non-native speakers have these two sounds in their languages, but both, especially [s], can be difficult to produce correctly.

- Whistling [s]: This high-pitched sound irritates listeners when they hear you speak into a microphone or on a teleconference call.
    - ***Correction:*** Move your tongue tip lower and away from your upper teeth. Keep moving it slowly until you lower the pitch and the whistling stops.
- Hissing: Speakers who hiss may be producing the correct sound, but they are holding the sound far too long.
    - ***Correction:*** Reduce the breath pressure. Don't emphasize the sound. Don't hang on to the sound too long.
- Omission of [s] or [z]: Often Asian and other language speakers fail to sound the [s] and [z] in the middle and at the end of words.
    - ***Correction:*** Speak more slowly and exaggerate the sounds until you get in the habit of saying them.

Contrast Pairs:

[s]	[z]	[s]	[z]
sip	zip	loose	lose
sink	zinc	advice	advise
sewn	zone	close	close [verb]
sue	zoo	ceasing	seizing
face	faze	racing	raising
grace	graze	sipper	zipper

Words at Work:

	Beginning		*Middle*	*End*
	system	[s]	assume	release
	central		proceed	surface
	cycle		instruct	process
	schedule		receive	address
	stock		describe	networks
	stability		essential	statements
	zone	[z]	example	confuse
	zigzag		visible	please
	zircon		reasonable	believes
	Zurich		resume	rings
	zero		music	approves
	zipper		noisy	itemize

Words with the letter s where the consonant is silent.

i<u>s</u>land debri<u>s</u> Illinoi<u>s</u> chassi<u>s</u> corp<u>s</u> Arkansa<u>s</u>

Other words you encounter with silent **s**:

______ ______ ______ _____

Practice Sentences for [s] and [z]

1 The security guard asked visitors to sign in at the desk.
2. The bus was full of commuters headed for their office buildings.
3. Insurance against loss is a major business expense.
4. The successful sales force won a trip to the South Sea Islands.
5. Our brainstorming sessions resulted in several new ideas.
6. Broken hoses on the assembly line can cause problems.
7. A press release announced our decision to sell a new system.
8. Each process change requires an analysis of several options.
9. Sam's supervisor requested that he instruct his coworkers.
10. The silo was full of maize harvested last season.
11. We have zero tolerance for drugs in our workplace.
12. Many Spanish speakers in Mexico also speak native dialects.

Difficult blends: The key to mastering these difficult blends is to first say each phoneme slowly and separately, and then pull the word together.

Examples: sss.....tripe ss....tripe s...tripe s..tripe s.tripe stripe

[str]	[skr]	[sts]	[sp]	[dz]
strike	scrub	insists	Hispanic	boards
instruct	scrap	guests	inspire	records
straight	script	lists	specific	codes
strong	screen	rusts	special	builds
instrument	scratch	wrists	aspect	bids
abstract	describe	resists	spare	rides
construct	scramble	dusts	spring	confides
structure	scroll	blasts	spiral	roads

Pronunciation Rule for the Final Letter *s*

The final letter *s* is pronounced either [s] or [z] when the **s** is added to a word to make it plural or to make it a 3rd person singular verb. The following rule will help you remember which sound to make.

- If the final sound of the original word is voiceless, make the voiceless [s].
  Examples: parts loops walks beliefs mouths
- If the final sound of the original word is voiced, make the voiced [z].
  Examples: plans boards emails stores names
- If the original word ends in the sound [s], [z], [ʃ], [ʒ], [tʃ] or [dʒ], add another syllable - either [ɛz] or [əz].
  Examples: misses pleases washes researches garages edges

♫ **Intonation:** Repeat the following phrases, some of which are American idioms. Emphasize the accented syllable to add rhythm and interest.

spills the béans
a snáke in the grass
a dozen red róses
boxes of bóoks

a nose for néws
sets an exámple
busy as twó bees
a bag of trícks

thirsty as a spónge
social secúrity
a sunset in Sumátra
zebra's strípes

[ʃ - ʒ]

► **Lesson 8**

Place of Articulation: tip and sides of the tongue

Classification: [ʃ] voiceless
[ʒ] voiced

Sentences: [ʃ] I spent the last <u>sh</u>are of my pen<u>s</u>ion in <u>Ch</u>icago, the na<u>ti</u>on's windy city.

[ʒ] A ca<u>s</u>ual meeting in a gara<u>ge</u> between two vi<u>si</u>onary explorers led to a trea<u>s</u>ure hunt in Malay<u>si</u>a.

Production: To make [ʃ], open your mouth slightly and separate your lips and teeth. Raise the sides of your tongue against the upper molars [back teeth], and point the front of your tongue up and just behind the gum ridge. Force out air.

To make [ʒ], add voice.

Be aware of these Problems with [ʃ] and [ʒ]

- A hissing sound can occur when producing [ʃ].
    - **Correction**: Push the tongue against the sides of your teeth. Practice making a firm contact between the inside upper teeth and tongue.
- Most non-native speakers can produce the sounds. Confusion occurs, however, in knowing whether to pronounce the last syllable in some words as [ʃ] or as [ʒ]. Unfortunately, there is no rule, but you can use the IPA to note the pronunciation of new or confusing words.
- For many speakers, the sound [ʃ] is often confused with the sounds [s] or [tʃ]. Practice the contrast pairs to help you distinguish the sounds.
    - **Correction**: The tongue position is critical. The tongue is more relaxed for [s] than for [ʃ]. The tongue tip does not touch the gum ridge when producing [ʃ], as it does for [tʃ].

Contrast Pairs:

[ʃ]	[s]	[ʃ]	[tʃ]
shore	sore	share	chair
short	sort	lash	latch
shell	sell	ship	chip
sheet	seat	cash	catch
shuttle	subtle	mush	much
crash	crass	mash	match
shock	sock	shop	chop
shingle	single	shatter	chatter
bash	bass	marsh	march
shield	sealed	shows	chose
shed	said	dish	ditch
shine	sign	crush	crutch

Words at Work:

	Beginning	*Middle*	*End*
[ʃ]	shovel	discussion	Spanish
	shape	commercial	establish
	sugar	fashionable	slash
	shatter	education	varnish
	Shanghai	motion	foolish
	chauffeur	brushed	rush
	chef	racial	mustache
	sure	conscious	embellish
	shrink	assure	refresh
[ʒ] *middle/end*	measure	version	prestige
	confusion	abrasion	sabotage
	erosion	decision	garage

Practice Sentences for [ʃ] and [ʒ]

1. Our distribution department is shipping chips to Russia.
2. Special machinery is necessary to grind the parts in our garage.
3. Showers were installed as a safety precaution in the factory.
4. Sales of shocking pink shoes have skyrocketed!
5. English education is becoming widespread in Asia.
6. An electrical short could cause the systems to crash.
7. Jacques made a decision to shut down his flower shop.
8. The manufacturing division shows signs of increased profits.
9. The issue before our committee concerns insurance.
10. The CEO gave a speech on the occasion of our expansion.
11. The latch to the heat chamber shouldn't be opened.

♫ **Intonation:** Repeat the following phrases. Emphasize the accented syllables to add rhythm and interest to your voice.

Dánish pástry	Rússian cáviar	Énglish Chánnel
Swédish sáuna	Túrkish báth	Pérsian cárpet
Ásian réstaurant	Fínnish masságe	Maláysian Península
Írish línen	Yíddish lánguage	Scóttish híghlands

[h]

▶ **Lesson 9**

Place of Articulation: vocal cords

Classification: voiceless

Sentence: <u>H</u>enry was kicked by a <u>h</u>orse in <u>H</u>olland.

Production: Your tongue should rest on the bottom of your mouth. Open your mouth and tighten your vocal cords as if you are going to whisper. Force air out your mouth, but don't let it escape through your nose.

Be Aware of these Problems with [h]

- Native French speakers and others may have trouble with this sound because the sound is not prevalent their languages. Otherwise, very few problems exist. It's one of the earliest sounds American children learn.
- Be aware of words containing the letter ***h*** in which the sound [h] isn't pronounced. Examples: **heir, honest, exhaust, honorary, herb**

Words at Work:

Beginning	*Middle*
human	inhale
rehearse	hardware
anyhow	unheard
hertz	perhaps
hurry	prehistoric
host	ad hoc
hamburger	coherent
humor	overhaul
hand held	offhand
highway	mishap
huge	uphold
haphazard	behind

Practice Sentences for [h]

1. High-tech companies value human creativity.
2. Health and harmony are keys to a long life.
3. Many happy endings have been filmed in Hollywood.
4. Huge hero sandwiches are popular with hungry handymen.
5. Who helped install the heater in the house?
6. The executive hosted a party in his high-rise apartment.
7. I said hello to Harold in the hallway, but he didn't hear me.
8. The hardware overheated, but it was not harmed.
9. Help yourself to more ham and hot tamales.
10. Harbors often have lighthouses to help ships in the night.
11. Honesty is behavior that we uphold at our company.
12. The hero saved the whole world from harm.

§ **Tongue Twisters:** These sentences provide additional practice for all of the fricative sounds. Read through the sentences several times quietly, and then try them aloud.

1. A very flexible plastic can curve with verve.
2. Clouds thickened as the gathering storm thundered in from the north.
3. Summer can mean lazy days sipping sugary soda on the seashore.
4. A massage is a most memorable experience in a beige garage.
5. Perhaps Harry's hunger made him heartily inhale his hat.
6. The zebras, seals and snakes seemed uneasy in the same cage at the zoo.
7. Because Zachary was rushed, he spilled his soup all over his suit.
8. March churns out chilly weather in Chicago and across Michigan.
9. Sue saw a shipment of zippers that needed to be sewn onto blouses.
10. A funny valentine is a favorite way to make a friend laugh.
11. His shined shoes shone against the shimmering summer street.
12. Judith's birthday party is on the third Thursday of the month.

►◄ **Dialogue:** Practice the following dialogue. In addition to numerous words containing fricative sounds from this chapter, you'll encounter American idioms and informal speech patterns.

The Staff Meeting

Chair: I've received instructions from the VP to explore several of our new initiative ideas.

Sharon: Super. I'm sure we can capture market share very fast.

Franco: Never assume a thing unless we show these ideas can result in a stream of new products.

Kathy: Okay, then let's define our scope and evaluate what's realistic.

Franco: For a start, let's list the absolutes to assure our success.

Van: I think the research phase is essential, though costly.

Sharon: Not necessarily. We've got resources in San Francisco.

Chair: You're suggesting a cross-discipline effort?

Sharon: Sure. Let's share resources with our subsidiary on the West Coast.

Van: I'll phone my friend who's involved with research out there.

Franco: Hold on. You're all jumping to conclusions. Putting the cart before the horse, so to speak.

Chair: Good point, Franco. Let's brainstorm options and then set up a process.

Chapter Four
The "Glides"
[Laterals]

[w] [r] [l] [j]

Glides are consonant sounds that are made when you move the articulators in the mouth from one position to another. You should hear a continuous movement of sound as you produce the glide.

[w]

Place of Articulation: lips

Classification: voiced

Note: We will not distinguish the voiceless [ʍ] from the voiced [w]. [ʍ] is not widely used in American English.

Sentence: <u>O</u>ne of the <u>w</u>arehouses <u>qu</u>ickly filled with <u>w</u>atermelons.

Production: Purse your lips. Raise the back of your tongue toward the roof of your mouth, but don't touch. As you blow air out, make a voiced sound. It's important to keep your mouth slightly open while you're blowing.

Be Aware of these Problems with [w]

- The sound [w] is often mispronounced by many people, including native speakers of German, Turkish, Hindi, Tamil and Urdu. The sound [v] is incorrectly substituted.
  - **Correction**: Use a mirror to check that your lips are pursed for [w], and that the teeth are ***not*** touching the lip [even on the inside of the lip].

Contrast Pairs:

[w]	[v]	[w]	[v]
wine	vine	we	V
Walt	vault	wail	veil
went	vent	while	vial
wet	vet	weal	veal
weird	veered	wiper	viper
wiser	visor	wile	vile
worse	verse	wow	vow
rowed	roved	mooing	moving
grew	groove	stow	stove
rower	rover	wane	vane
Y	vie	wary	vary
waltz	vaults	rowing	roving

Words at Work:

Beginning	*Middle*
website	liquid
wavelength	firmware
white paper	sandwich
women	network
welcome	reward
weather	frequent
Wednesday	requirement
whenever	bandwidth
welder	wristwatch
weave	dwindle
worldwide	request
window	worthwhile

Words with the letter w where the consonant is silent.

S<u>w</u>ord <u>w</u>rist <u>w</u>rite <u>w</u>hole <u>w</u>rong <u>w</u>rench

Other words you encounter with silent **w**:

______ ______ ______ ______

Practice Sentences for [w]

1. We want everyone to feel welcome at work.
2. Please forward that email to our Wisconsin customer.
3. Wayne enjoys surfing the World Wide Web.
4. That radio frequency can be heard halfway around the world.
5. Highway workers wave signs to slow down drivers.
6. The software we requested is arriving by midweek.
7. The supply of hardware components has dwindled.
8. Our headquarter building is wired for extra bandwidth.
9. Please wait to ask questions in the Q&A session.
10. One of our wisest employees has been here for a quarter century.
11. The weather in Wellington, New Zealand, can be wild.
12. The boss always welcomes requests for overtime.

♫ Rising and Falling Inflection

Inflection means a change in pitch that occurs within a spoken word. It's as though your voice is gliding up or down. For example, if you say *Yes* ↗ with a rising inflection, you might be answering the phone, or acknowledging someone's question at a meeting.

If you say *Yes* ↘ with a falling inflection, you are responding positively to a question. Your response might be neutral or forceful, depending on how much your voice falls and how loudly you speak.

◙ **Exercise 1**: Read the following dialogue. Glide your voice up and down in order to express feeling. What might Walt and Van be discussing?

Walt: How many? ↗

Van: Twelve. ↘

Walt: Why? ↗

Van: It's not worth buying more. ↘

Walt: Really? ↗

Van: Yes. ↘

Walt: I don't (→) agree. ↘

Van: You're free to disagree. ↘

Walt: Sure, it's a free country. ↘

Van: Okay, then you'll sell me twelve? ↗

Walt: Yes. →

Van: Thanks. ↘

◙ Exercise No 2: Inflection with Interrogative Questions

Interrogative questions usually begin with the 5 Ws and an H:
Who, What, Where, When, Why, and How. Because these questions call for an "informational" answer, not a Yes/No response, your voice falls at the end of such a question.

For example: Where did you put the box of files? ↘

Why is the moving van parked at the door? ↘

◙ Practice: Read the following sentences.

Remember to move your voice up down within the sentence, and then glide it down at the end of the sentence.

1. Who's visiting the office today?
2. When will we get together again?
3. Who left this wrench on my workbench?
4. How can I help you?
5. What is your favorite weekend activity?
6. Where in the world have I misplaced my watch?
7. Who's joining us for lunch?
8. How can we solve this problem?
9. What's happening on Wednesday?
10. Where can I find a doctor?
11. What's on this week's calendar?
12. When is the launch date?

How to Speak with Authority

Too often in the business world, people lack authority and certainty when they speak. One reason is the irritating habit of raising the voice at the end of a statement. Such a habit makes you sound uncertain, hesitant, or immature.

To correct that habit and gain strength and authority:

- Always glide your voice down at the end of a statement.
- Glide your voice down when asking an interrogative question.
- Glide your voice down at the end of a series in a sentence.
- Women, whose voices are naturally higher, must be particularly aware of not raising their voices at the end of statements. Otherwise they may sound unsure of themselves.

[r] ► Lesson 11

Place of Articulation: tip and sides of the tongue

Classification: voiced

Sentence: Rosaria drove for an hour before the traffic increased.

Production: Open your mouth slightly and protrude your lips. Raise your tongue and curl it behind the gum ridge ***without touching the roof of the mouth***. Spread the sides of the tongue so that they touch the inside of the upper teeth.

Be Aware of these Problems with [r]

- [r] is one of the most troublesome sounds in English, and one of the last sounds that children master. Recognize that it can be a hard sound to say.
- [r] is sounded differently in various regions of the U.S., and among non-native speakers throughout the world. Native speakers of Spanish, Italian French and Portuguese, as well as some speakers of Irish and British English, often "trill" the [r]. They tap the tongue lightly and quickly against the gum ridge when saying [r].
    - **Correction:** To avoid the "trill", keep your tongue from touching anything as you produce [r].
- Some speakers substitute [w] for [r].
    - **Correction**: Don't purse your lips when saying [r].
- Asian language speakers may substitute [l] for [r]. Thus, they may say *lip* when they want to say **rip**.
    - **Correction**: make sure that your tongue tip does not touch the gum ridge when making [r].

Contrast Pairs:

[r]	[w]	[r]	[l]
run	won	read	lead
rave	wave	royal	loyal
round	wound	rim	limb
rate	weight	cramp	clamp
rise	wise	grass	glass
more	mow	fire	file
roared	rowed	erect	elect
rage	wage	crutch	clutch
rife	wife	row	low
reared	weird	rink	link
raced	waist	tire	tile
ring	wing	rater	later

Words at Work:

Beginning	*Middle*	*End*
robot	curious	entire
respond	perform	square
random	service	registrar
radial	word	power
write	distribute	clear
ramp	birthday	elsewhere
remote	partner	software
restrict	stringent	peer
round	warehouse	explore
receive	urgent	inspire
region	electronic	ensure
robust	practical	ladder

Practice Sentences for [r]

1. Robotics is really the wave of the future.
2. Brazil is certainly much warmer than Norway.
3. A burger and fries is a popular American fast food order.
4. Let's wrap up the board retreat by Friday.
5. I took a crash course in racecar driving.
6. The resources for more R&D will arrive in April.
7. A worldwide shortage of erasers could drive up the price.
8. "Race for the Cure" raises money for cancer research.
9. The jet stream brought pouring rain to the Northwest.
10. A robust agricultural industry means happier workers.
11. Please credit us for the returned products.
12. Rao gave a well-received presentation to his team.

Troublesome Blends

[pr]	[br]	[tr]	[dr]
project	broad	traffic	drive
probe	calibrate	attract	hundred
proof	brand	entrance	drag
April	abrupt	training	quadrant
prompt	brace	trend	dry run
express	bridge	electric	address
principle	breath	transit	dredge
problem	bright	tracker	withdraw
approach	abrasive	truck	foundry
process	library	trusted	drain

[fr]	[kr]	[gr]	[rz]
fraction	create	diagram	chairs
frequent	increase	agreed	features
infringe	crunch	grade	workers
frame	micro	regret	adheres
French	recruit	gross	explores
friend	scroll	grind	vectors
freeze	acrid	graduate	pliers
Africa	concrete	hungry	peers
affront	credible	angry	stores
frustrated	scrap	grain	soars
fragile	secret	gratitude	bankers
freeware	crash	grasp	stairs

More Practice Sentences for [r]

1. I'd rather hear your response before I resolve the issue.
2. Roberto has flown in from Puerto Rico.
3. If you strike the keyboard with force you'll break it.
4. Drive four miles and turn right at the corner.
5. Our products are distributed worldwide.
6. Many years ago all roads led to Rome.
7. Contact the personnel department if you have problems.
8. The weather is stormy, but our crew is still working hard.
9. Which market sector should we address this year?
10. My workstation is near the cafeteria.
11. Entrepreneurs sometimes have a "rags to riches" story.
12. A career in dentistry requires steady hands.

♫ **Intonation:** Repeat the following phrases, some of which are American idioms. Emphasize the accented syllable to add rhythm and interest.

pair of róbots	reckless dríver	pouring ráin
péarl of great príce	older bróther	put down róots
rúles of the róad	round róbin	red ríbbon
parallel pórt	creative wríter	stormy wéather

[l]

▶ **Lesson 12**

Place of Articulation: tongue and upper gum ridge

Classification: voiced

Sentence: Luis placed a call to his family in Lisbon.

Production: Place the tip of your tongue lightly against your upper gum ridge. Keep the sides of your tongue down to allow air to flow over the sides. Your lips should be wide enough to slip the tip of your finger between your teeth. Then produce sound.

Be Aware of these Problems with [l]

- Two pronunciations of [l] occur in English: the "dark" [l] and the "clear" [l]. The "clear" [l] appears at the beginning of a word as in lap, light, leave. The "dark" [l] is produced slightly further back in the mouth, but still on the gum ridge. It appears at the end of words as in feel, pull, pale.
    - Make sure that your tongue touches the gum ridge for both sounds!
- Some speakers substitute [w] for [l] at the end of words. Example: *seow* for **seal**.
    - **Correction**: Watch yourself in a mirror. Make sure you are not collapsing your lips at the end of the word. ***Only the tongue should move as it curls up and touches the gum ridge.***
- If you are an Asian language speaker, you may have difficulty with [l]. Often speakers produce the sound with the tongue tip curled behind but not touching the gum ridge. If you do that, you'll produce a [r] sound.
    - **Correction**: Touch your tongue tip to the gum ridge!

Contrast:

"clear" [l]	"dark" [l]	"clear [l]	"dark" [l]
late	tale	lab	ball
leap	peal	lug	gull
lost	stall	late	tail
least	steal	lean	kneel

Contrast Pairs:

[l]	[r]	[l]	[r]
light	right	flee	free
lash	rash	liver	river
legion	region	glass	grass
lamp	ramp	bill	beer
clash	crash	dial	dire
clutch	crutch	filing	firing
glimmer	grimmer	lag	rag
lobe	robe	climb	crime
lied	ride	clown	crown
lock	rock	fleas	freeze
role	roar	mile	mire
lead	read	leak	reek

Words at Work:

Beginning	*Middle*	*End*
laugh	dollar	digital
launch	global	hotel
legal	silicon	schedule
leader	eleven	level
length	hallway	capital
local	colleague	wheel
liability	excellent	fuel
labor	timeline	optimal
lease	wireless	cyclical
location	always	barrel
legitimate	bulletin	commercial
lateral	exclude	probable

How to Speak Like an American

How to Pronounce [l] after the sounds [t], [d], and [n]

little ladle funnel

To pronounce these [l] combinations as Americans do, keep your tongue touching the gum ridge after producing [t, d, n]. Simply drop the sides of the tongue as you produce the [l] sound.

Practice:	little	pedal	tunnel	battle	settle	saddle
	bottle	handle	panel	puddle	Seattle	channel

Practice Sentences for [l]

1. Please walk slowly down the long, narrow hallway.
2. Santa Clara is in the heart of Silicon Valley.
3. Lee lives close to work, so he rides his bicycle.
4. We must allocate more dollars to the lab.
5. All the players on the football team ran for the goal.
6. The eldest member of the local council caught a cold.
7. Local police responded quickly to the fire alarm.
8. Lola greeted her colleagues in the lobby of the hotel.
9. A panel of legal experts ruled on the case.
10. Let's table the idea until we have additional data.
11. The last validation experiment failed miserably.
12. I like the new, longer look of the console.

♫ **Intonation**: Repeat the following phrases, some of which are American idioms. Emphasize the accented syllable for rhythm and interest.

líve and lét live	little by líttle	the smell of gárlic
tall in the sáddle	Long Ísland	live Maine lóbster
let's call it a dáy	let's have lúnch	fall in lóve
double pláy	legal éagle	sleepless in Seáttle

[j]

▶ **Lesson 13**

Place of Articulation: front of the tongue and the hard palate

Classification: voiced

Sentence: The millionaire distributed his wealth to poor youths.

Production: Open your mouth slightly and raise the back of your tongue. Curl the tongue tip down and behind your lower front teeth. Don't touch the back of your tongue to the roof of your mouth. Then pull your lips back slightly as you produce voice, and glide the tongue and lips to the next sound.

Be Aware of these Problems with [j]

- Some native Spanish speakers and others interchange [dʒ] and [j]. Thus, the word **yard** becomes *jarred*, and the word **yes** becomes the non-word *jes*.
  - **Correction:** Make sure your tongue tip is touching behind the ***lower*** front teeth. Do not raise the tongue tip, only the back of the tongue.
- Note that the phonetic symbol can be confusing for this sound. The symbol [j] is often the sound for the letter *y*, while the phonetic symbol [dʒ] may represent words with the letter *j*, which looks like but is not the symbol [j]. It's important to think of sound, not letters.

Contrast Pairs:

[j]	[dʒ]	[j]	[dʒ]
yet	jet	Yale	jail
yellow	Jello	yolk	joke
yawn	John	yaw	jaw
yak	Jack	use	juice
year	jeer	yard	jarred
yacht	jot	yam	jam

Practice Sentences for [j]

1. Union Station is a popular arrival place for travelers.
2. The employee from Uganda stayed for several years.
3. John used his beautiful yacht for business.
4. Distribution of a hundred units took until Tuesday.*
5. At the university I studied the work of Carl Jung.
6. Yoko was promoted from junior to senior executive.
7. The New* York Yankees have won many World Series.
8. One of the institutes* for health suggests a diet of yogurt.
9. If you go to Utah, make sure to see the rock monuments.
10. The European euro is a major world currency.
11. Add onions to the stew* for more flavor.
12. The yield on popular treasury bonds is universally high.

Note: * indicates an alternative pronunciation. The vowel sound in these words can be pronounced [u] or [j]. Thus, the word **news** can be pronounced [nuz], which is preferable, or [njuz].

§ **Tongue Twisters for the glide sounds**: Practice each sentence aloud. You may need to slow down at first in order to pronounce all the sounds. Then try to say the sentence correctly without hesitating.

1. I'd rather be rid of radishes that rise up in the garden.
2. The Wednesday weather report is wrong more often than right.
3. Purple leather appears lovely to the planetary people of Lyre.
4. Larry has yet to travel by tunnel under the English Channel.
5. Regional travel by helium balloon will someday be normal.
6. A yield of triangular yellow units was distributed in New York.
7. Youngsters usually yell when toys are beyond their reach.
8. Yellow-less egg yolks are usually unpopular among youths.
9. The red thread on Rachael's dress unraveled in an hour.
10. Laura liked licorice-flavored lamb in late afternoon.
11. Wilted wisteria wandered quietly along the wall.
12. When will Walter quit the wrestling squad?

►◄ Dialogue:

On the Production Line

Len: I've called this meeting to update you on the line problem that occurred yesterday.

Yun: What went wrong? I saw the yellow caution ribbon.

Len: Luckily no one was injured, but we were all worried.

Darrell: Well, tell us what happened.

Len: Weaver, the tool owner, was walking the line as usual when he heard a roar.

Larry: Like the loud rumbling I heard last week?

Darrell: A false alarm, remember?

Len: Yeah, but unfortunately this time it turned out to be a chemical leak.

Yun: Did Weaver follow procedures?

Len: Perfectly. He alerted the emergency response unit.

Yun: So the line was cleared right away?

Len: Yes. It proves that our safety drills are familiar, and useful.

▣ **Idea for a Conversation:** Have you ever had an unusual idea that could make you a millionaire? Perhaps becoming rich is only a dream, but organizations often provide rewards and recognition to employees who come up with good ideas.

Think about your choice of words, as well as your pronunciation, when you share a good idea.

Word Wise:

Write down troublesome words you have encountered at work, or anywhere. They may be words you mispronounced or were hesitant to say, and thus you limited your ability to express yourself. Use the IPA to note the pronunciation.

Start with these particularly difficult words containing [r] and [l].

parallel ____________
particularly ____________
probably ____________
library ____________
wireless ____________
world ____________

____________	____________	____________	____________
____________	____________	____________	____________
____________	____________	____________	____________
____________	____________	____________	____________
____________	____________	____________	____________
____________	____________	____________	____________

↓

Ideas pass through three periods:

– It can't be done.

– It probably can be done, but it's not worth doing.

–I knew it was a good idea all along!

~ Arthur C. Clarke, author *2001: A Space Odyssey*

Chapter Five
The "Nasals"

[m , n, ŋ]

The three nasal sounds, as the descriptor indicates, are formed by directing the breath stream through the nose. Sound resonates in the mouth but is blocked by the tongue or the lips, and so the sound is directed out through the nose.

[m]

▶ **Lesson 14**

Place of Articulation: lips

Classification: voiced

Sentence: Autumn is a time to remember calm summer months.

Production: Close your lips. Keep your teeth slightly apart and your tongue relaxed as you force air through your nose.

Be Aware of this Problem with [m]

Few problems exist with the sound [m]. It is one of the first sounds a child learns. Think of the word for Mother in your native language. Chances are it begins with [m].

- The only problem occurs when speakers fail to pronounce [m] in the middle or at the end of words because they are speaking too quickly.
    - **Correction:** Slow down and put your lips together for [m].

Words at Work:

Beginning	*Middle*	*End*
medium	pneumatic	paradigm
manual	eliminate	platform
method	administer	diagram
microscope	preeminent	palm
multiple	tremendous	column
malfunction	import	capitalism
massive	schematic	mainstream
mechanical	teamwork	flextime
mistake	temperature	algorithm
maintenance	similar	self-esteem
mouse	remote	synonym
module	embed	item

Practice Sentences for [m]

1. Some people march to a different drummer.
2. Mira composes music on her computer.
3. Mohammed performed admirably on his exam.
4. Always document your method so others can emulate you.
5. The numerous choices of ice cream tempted me.
6. Michael heads the team that's making the modifications.
7. Chemists must mix elements without a mishap.
8. Moshe's job is to manually adjust the temperature.
9. Humans are multiplying at an amazing rate.
10. Mr. Maloney took his camera to Mt. Fuji.
11. Our automobile got stuck in the mud during the rainstorm.
12. The Malaysian employees emphasized customer service.

♫ **Intonation:** Repeat the following phrases, some of which are American idioms. Emphasize the accented syllable to add rhythm and interest to your voice.

súmmer time	customer compláint	March of Dímes
númbers game	fámily man	prime mínister
month of Máy	mix and mátch	Roman cólumn
major próblem	. cóm	Mississippi múd

[n]

▶ **Lesson 15**

Place of Articulation: tip of the tongue and gum ridge

Classification: voiced

Sample Sentence: The kitche<u>n</u> cabi<u>n</u>et held a <u>n</u>umber of <u>kn</u>ives.

Production: Place your tongue tip on the upper gum ridge. Push the sides of your tongue against the inner edges of your upper teeth. Then direct air through your nose.

Problems with the sound [n]

Few problems exist with [n]. However, some speakers omit the [n] sound when it comes before a consonant or before the letter ***d***, as in the word **round**.

- **Correction**: Touch your tongue to the gum ridge for [n].

Words at Work:

Beginning	*Middle*	*End*
notify	economy	conclusion
natural	uniform	remain
ninety	synthesize	loan
nominate	environment	medicine
national	boundary	dial tone
normalize	fortune	abandon
north	earnings	mention
nest egg	enhance	human
negative	tension	fusion
nanosecond	download	screen
knowledge	funded	operation
North Atlantic	Internet	constrain

Practice Sentences for [n]

1. Visionaries are always looking for the new, new thing.
2. Money management is a necessary part of financial planning.
3. No one ordered lunch until Anwar thought of it.
4. I found a new knapsack on the Net.
5. Accountants need to balance the books.
6. We know next to nothing about the planet Saturn.
7. Hindi is spoken in many parts of India.
8. Nancy noticed the politician from the Netherlands.
9. The Santa Ana winds blew across Southern California.
10. The foundation granted the scientist enough money.
11. Insurance is mandatory for a new enterprise.

♫ **Intonation**: Repeat the following phrases, some of which are American idioms. Emphasize the accented syllable to add rhythm and interest.

kníck knacks	in tune with the tímes	financial néws
ónce in awhile	knock on wóod	North by Northwést
natural seléction	next generátion	next to nóthing
United Nátions	in the knów	a nose for néws

[ŋ]

▶ **Lesson 16**

Place of Articulation: back of the tongue and soft palate

Classification: voiced

Sentence: I'm a<u>n</u>xious to visit the ba<u>n</u>k in Beiji<u>ng</u>.

Production: Raise the back of your tongue and touch the lowered soft palate, as if you're about to say [g]. Then produce voice and direct the air through your nose to make [ŋ].

Be Aware of this Problem with [ŋ]

Very few problems exist with this sound. The only difficulty is when speakers drop the [ŋ] at the end of words and instead say [n]. Example: *goin'* instead of **going**.
Be careful to enunciate the last sound.

Contrast Pairs:

[ŋ]	[n]	[ŋ]	[n]
tongue	ton	singing	sinning
wing	win	banged	banned
rung	run	clang	clan
king	kin	fanged	fanned
winged	wind	banger	banner
tang	tan	things	thins
stung	stun	wingless	winless
long	lawn	rungs	runs
gong	gone	pinging	pinning
ding	din	hanged	hand
bang	ban	sung	sun
singer	sinner	panged	panned

In the following words, be sure to say [k] after the [ŋ].

think	banker	anchor	jinx	planks	strength
inkjet	junk	bankrupt	thanks	ankle	length

Pronunciation Rule for [ŋ] and [ŋg]

- Many non-native speakers become confused by English spelling and are unsure of when to use [ŋ] alone and when to follow [ŋ] with [g]. Here are rules that will help you choose which sound to use.
- Say [ŋ] when the word ends in the letters *ng*. Examples: **ring, sang, going**
- Say [ŋ] when the letters *ng* or another suffix is added to a root word that ends in *ng*. For example: **banging**, **singer, kingly**
- Say [ŋ] + [g] when the letters *ng* are within the original word and are therefore a necessary part of the word. Examples: **finger, hunger, language**
- Exceptions: Say [ŋ] + [g] in the comparative and superlative forms of words such as: **young, younger, youngest**, or **strong, stronger, strongest**

Practice Sentences for [ŋ]

1. Balancing the books is basic to good accounting practices.
2. I always feel hungry after eating junk food.
3. The ship anchored in the harbor in Hong Kong.
4. A thinker needs time for dreaming and meditating.
5. Streaming video reached employees in Bangladesh.
6. The English usually drink tea in the morning.
7. My printer is out of ink, so I think I'll head for the store.
8. The fishnets became entangled with the evening's catch.
9. The angle of the tool is important when etching.
10. Many buildings surround the harbor in Penang.
11. After booting up the system, Chang began working.
12. Eliminating defects is the key to making a profit.

♫ **Intonation**: Repeat the following phrases, some of which are American idioms. Emphasize the accented syllables to add rhythm and interest to your voice.

singing in the ráin
skúnk works
thanks a lót
léarning curve
morning páper
stronger than íron
hungry as a hórse
Anchors awáy!
thínk tank
a red hérring
bánk account
Star-Spangled Bánner

Pronunciation Tip: Stress Prefixes. De-emphasize suffixes.

A **prefix** is a group of letters added in front of a word to change the meaning of the word – often to its opposite. Therefore, a ***prefix receives emphasis*** because it is important that your meaning be clear. Common prefixes in business include: ***un, mis, de, non, ir, in, re, pre.*** Say the following words. Each has a double stress – the prefix and another syllable in the word.

nónfúnctional	míscommunicátion	úninténtional
mísguíded	ré-ímage	írrégular
ínescápable	únéducated	únnátural
ínvóluntary	díssátisfied	únlóaded
únimáginable	ré-dígitalize	préáuthorized
réfórmat	úndócumented	íllégal
íllógical	mísinfórm	úncharacterístic
nón-restríctive	mísapprópriate	súbzéro

A **suffix** is a group of letters attached to the end of a word. Suffixes are a grammatical necessity because they indicate usage – verb tense, noun, adjective, or adverb. However, they do not alter the root meaning of the word. Therefore, ***suffixes are not stressed.*** Suffixes include: ***tion, able, ment, ing, ence, ive, ic, an, ous, ity.*** The stress comes on another syllable, often the syllable just before the suffix. Practice these words commonly used at work.

assórtment	electrónic	validátion
equípment	synthesízer	recéivable
resílience	díctionary	contróllable
propríetary	enháncement	functionálity
infórmative	abstráction	compilátion
standardizátion	cómfortable	advísable
partítion	reliabílity	idéntical
opportunístic	simultáneous	ímaging

Suggestion: When you hear someone use an unfamiliar or confusing word at work, place the stress mark [´] above the syllable in order to remember which syllable[s] should be stressed. ***Stress is very important.*** If you incorrectly stress a word, the listener may not understand you. Note: You will find additional exercises on Word Stress in **Chapter Six**.

►◄ Dialogue

At the Front Desk

Kim: [receptionist] Good morning, Mr. Neumann. Would you please sign in.

Neumann: May I have a pen? Thank you. It's nice to be back.

Kim: Ms. Anderson is running a little late. How was your flight from Germany?

Neumann: Uneventful, but long. My day began in France.

Kim: May I offer you coffee while you're waiting?

Neumann: Certainly, but as you know, we Europeans like it strong.

Kim: Yes, I know. Excuse me a moment while I grind some coffee beans.

Neumann: I'll make myself comfortable and glance at the newspapers.

Kim: You might enjoy viewing the new artwork in the waiting area.

Neumann: Those paintings are most interesting. Who's the artist?

Kim: He's an up-and-coming new painter from Hong Kong.

Neumann: Ah, here comes Ms. Anderson now.

Note: ***Mr.*** and ***Ms.*** are formal titles for addressing people you have just met, or people who are senior to you in an organization. In the United States people are very informal. Upon meeting you, they will often address you by your first name, and expect you to address them using their first names. However, throughout much of the rest of the world, formal titles are still common. The title ***Ms.*** [mɪz] refers to a woman who may or may not be married. Many American women now prefer to be addressed as ***Ms.***

Chapter Six
"Consonant Combos"
[Affricates]

[tʃ] and [dʒ]

The two sounds [tʃ] and [dʒ] are consonant combinations. Each one is a closely and rapidly blended combination of a plosive and a fricative sound. You begin with the plosive sound [t] or [d] and then merge it with the fricative [ʃ] or [ʒ].

[tʃ - dʒ]

▶ **Lesson 17**

Place of Articulation: tongue tip and upper gum ridge, the sides of the tongue, and the front part of the palate

Classification: [tʃ] voiceless
[dʒ] voiced

Sentence: [Both Sounds] Jiang manages a jewelry store that sells gold chains, so she naturally hears questions about cheap imitations.

Production: Open your mouth slightly and place the tip of your tongue against the gum ridge, as if you are going to say [t]. Touch the sides of the tongue against the side teeth. Then quickly release air pressure as you let a portion of your tongue tip leave the gum ridge. Although you begin with [t] you end with [ʃ].

To make [dʒ], do the same as above, but produce voice as soon as you feel your tongue touch the gum ridge.

Be Aware of these Problems with [tʃ] and [dʒ]

- The voiceless [tʃ] can be particularly difficult for Spanish speakers, as well as for those who speak Arabic, French German, Korean and Filipino. Those speakers may turn the sound into a [ʃ]. Thus, the word **chair** becomes *share*; and the word **kitchen** is incorrectly said as *kishen.*
    - **Correction**: You must say the [t] portion of the blend. Feel the tip of your tongue on the gum ridge as you pronounce the sound.

continued →

- The sound [dʒ] poses problems for non-native speakers whose first language is one of the Asian or Scandinavian languages, French, German, or Spanish, as well as other speakers. They turn the sound into [j]. Thus the word **John** becomes *yon*, and the word **manager** becomes *manayer*.
- Arabic and Hebrew speakers also have trouble with [dʒ] in the final position. Thus, the word **edge** is mispronounced *esh* or *ezh*.
  - **Correction:** You must say the [d] portion of the blend. Feel the tip of your tongue on the upper gum ridge. Take your time saying the sound. Practice the contrast pairs below.

Contrast Pairs:

[tʃ]	[dʒ]	[tʃ]	[dʒ]
batch	badge	chest	jest
chunk	junk	etch	edge
cheap	jeep	britches	bridges
choke	joke	chin	gin
search	surge	cherry	Jerry
etching	edging	cinch	singe
rich	ridge	perching	purging
chew	Jew	larch	large
lunch	lunge	char	jar
cheer	jeer	match	Madge
choice	Joyce	chugged	jugged
chinks	jinx	etches	edges

Contrast Pairs:

[tʃ]	[ʃ]	[dʒ]	[j]
chair	share	joke	yoke
chip	ship	jail	Yale
chew	shoe	jeer	year
chose	shows	jot	yacht
catch	cash	juice	use
leach	leash	jet	yet
cheese	she's	jam	yam
chin	shin	paging	paying
chore	shore	Jello	yellow
chop	shop	jarred	yard
cheat	sheet	hedge	hay
cheer	sheer	jaw	yaw

Words at Work:

	Beginning	*Middle*	*End*
[tʃ]	challenge	merchandise	patch
	choice	achievement	coach
	chamber	fracture	research
	champion	purchase	branch
	charge	factual	latch
	check up	actually	wrench
[dʒ]	generate	manager	package
	gender	strategic	pledge
	journal	regional	wage
	justify	educate	bridge
	genetics	budget	purge
	judgment	gradual	surge

Practice Sentences for [tʃ] and [dʒ]

1. The chair of the meeting handed out the agenda.
2. Charlie, the night watchman, checked everyone's badge.
3. My manager championed my project to the Vice President.
4. Judging by our sales, the new product is a gigantic success.
5. The questionable data made me recheck the budget.
6. The sky bridge between the buildings generated more traffic.
7. A communications coach can catch your speech errors.
8. All of us pledged to achieve our long-term strategy.
9. If you adjust the agenda, we'll have time for my budget report.
10. Engage your audience with a well-timed question.
11. The German tourist chose a budget car in Japan.
12. Chang showed genuine concern for my children.

♫ **Intonation:** Repeat the following phrases, some of which are American idioms. Emphasize the accented syllable to add rhythm and interest.

Frénch fries	virtual fáctory	strategic advántage
lóunge chair	órange juice	lúnch break
just in tíme	joint vénture	natural envíronment
under síege	búdget cuts	a matter of ínches

If you want to be listened to at work, you need to understand how to emphasize [stress] certain words in a sentence – those words that convey the special meaning of what you are saying. ***Stress involves making a key phrase or word louder or higher pitched than the other words in the sentence.***

Example: The manager told his team to prepare two reports.
The general stress pattern spoken at a moderate tone would be:
The mánager told his téam to prepáre two repórts.

Notice that a rhythm occurs. ***Nouns*** and ***verbs*** are generally emphasized because they are the primary conveyers of information and meaning. However, ***any word in a sentence may be stressed for clarity or emphasis.***

Now read the questions and answers again, this time strongly stressing the underlined word to signal your intended meaning. Continue to give moderate stress to the other nouns.

Q. Who told his team to prepare two reports?
A. The manager told his team to prepare two reports.

Q. Did the manager ask his team to prepare two reports?
A. The manager told his team to prepare two reports.

Q. Did the manager tell our team to prepare two reports?
A. The manager told his team to prepare two reports.

You get the idea. The objective is to allow your voice to move beyond a neutral place, and rid yourself of the monotonous tone that some non-native speakers use because they're self-conscious about their accents. Your coworkers will appreciate a clear, rhythmic voice. And they'll respond to your message!

◙ **Exercise**:

> ➢ First choose one a stress pattern for each sentence and read it aloud.
> ➢ Next, read the sentence again with a different pattern.

1. I really need a vacation.
2. That's on the agenda?
3. Where can I get one like yours?
4. Maria works a lot of overtime.
5. Tomorrow I'm buying a digital camera.
6. Meet my friends in the north cafeteria.
7. How do you think we should proceed?
8. Here's my first point.
9. I said May, not March.
10. Please give me two hours to finish.
11. If only I could win the raffle!
12. Which conference room have you booked?

Word stress is critical for effective communication at work.

Stress is nearly as important as sound production. Usually a word is considered mispronounced if you stress the wrong syllable. Equally important, your coworkers might not understand you if you fail to stress the word correctly.

Following are guidelines for stressing the correct syllable in a word:

1. When **two nouns are combined to form a single word, we usually stress the first noun more than the second one.** Read the following words, taking care to correctly stress the first syllable of the word:

software	overhead	underpass	notebook
startup	airplane	mainstream	download
waterproof	bandwidth	guideline	password
backspace	roadmap	letterhead	waterfront

2. More than **75% of two-syllable words** have their **stress on the first syllable**. Thus, if you don't know where the stress should be, take a guess on the first syllable. Remember, though, that in English there are no hard and fast rules.

prior	method	mortgage	active	process	vendor
audit	error	doctor	forty	market	issue
modern	optic	damage	digit	agent	service
science	hundred	journey	urban	icon	module

However, many two-syllable words such as these have a second-syllable stress.

enjoy	again	employ	proceed	remote	obtain
reverse	remove	ensure	assume	suppress	destroy

Once again you see how confusing English can be. Make sure to mark words you hear at work with a stress mark [′] so that in the future you will say them correctly.

__________ __________ __________ __________ __________
__________ __________ __________ __________ __________
__________ __________ __________ __________ __________
__________ __________ __________ __________ __________

3. Polysyllabic words [three or more syllables] **usually follow a pattern whereby the stressed syllable moves along the word as it lengthens**.

Pronounce the following words. The stressed syllable is noted.

phótograph	photógraphy	photográphic
próduct	prodúction	productívity
dífferent	differéntial	differentiátion
infórm	informátion	
depénd	dependabílity	
óccupy	occupátion	
mánage	managérial	
fínance	fináncial	
régular	regulárity	
ánxious	anxíety	
símple	simplícity	simplificátion
presént	presentátion	

English is a dynamic language. Each year thousands of words are added to the dictionary. New words emerge from various disciplines: business, medicine, science, the arts, sports. Other words begin as slang [informal and unconventional speech] and then gain widespread acceptance. The job of mastering English never ends, even for Americans. As you note new words, ask someone for a definition or look the word up in the dictionary. Those of you who have school-age children will certainly hear the latest slang from them!

"Speaking on your Feet"

Employees working in a team-oriented environment are often called upon to speak at meetings. At times there's no opportunity to prepare, so you have to "speak on your feet," an idiom that means to speak in the moment. When such an unplanned occasion arises, it is important to be as prepared as you can. Therefore, you will want to practice language for how you will respond. Below are some situations where your manager might ask you to speak on your feet.

Practice aloud, and ideally with a friend or colleague, how you would respond. Hear yourself use clear pronunciation and good vocabulary.

1. What's the update this week on your project?

____

2. How is our customer responding to our new product/service?

____

3. I don't understand how you'll solve the problem. Tell me again.

____

4. I hear there's a problem in the factory [or office]. What happened?

____

5. What responsibilities will you take on to move the project forward?

____

6. What do you think about this new idea?

____

►◄ **Dialogue**:

The Company Picnic

Jen: I'll watch the children while you get in line for the buffet.

George: Okay. I'll just check out our choices.

[*He returns*] There's chicken, turkey sausages, burgers, and vegetarian kabobs.

Jen: Get one of each, George. We can try them all and share.

George [goes and returns] Grab the plates. Quickly, before I drop everything! And here's juice for everyone.

Jen: You forgot the potato chips and the ketchup.

George: Oh, that's all junk food.

[They begin eating.]

Jen: George, what do they have for dessert?

George [goes/returns] Well, there's chocolate cake, chocolate chip cookies, and fudge brownies.

Jen: That'll do for the kids. But over there on that far table I also see wedges of watermelon and a big bowl of oranges.

George: I suppose you'd like a sample of each!

Jen: Yes, George. I'll take the kids down to the edge of the water and wait for you to bring us some dessert.

George: Sometimes I feel like a restaurant waiter, not a manager.

Jen: You're a great manager, George, but today your main job is to be a good father and husband.

Chapter Seven
Front Vowels

[i, ɪ, e/eɪ, ɛ, æ]

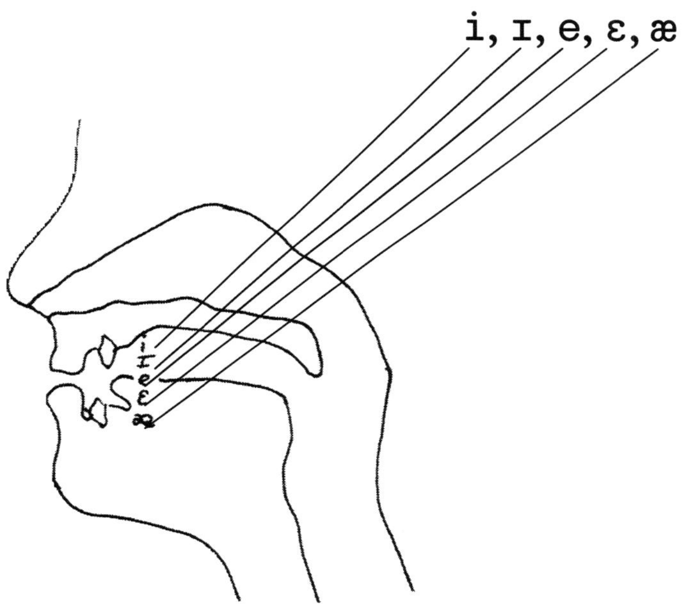

The front vowel sounds are produced by placing the tongue forward in the mouth.

Note: <u>All</u> vowels are classified as *voiced.*

[i] ▶ Lesson 19

Sentence: The k<u>ey</u> p<u>ie</u>ce of mach<u>i</u>nery that w<u>e</u> n<u>ee</u>d is not ch<u>ea</u>p.

Spelling combinations for the sound [i]

e as in **we**	**ea** as in **cheap**	**i** as in **machinery**
ee as in **need**	**ie** as in **piece**	**ei** as in **seize**
y as in **floppy**	**eo** as in **people**	**ey** as in **key**

Production: To produce the long vowel [i], open your mouth slightly and spread your lips across your teeth, as if you are going to smile. Arch the sides of the tongue high. Tense and point the tip of the tongue toward the lower front teeth.

Be Aware of these Problems with [i]

- While the sound [i] is easy to produce, speakers from nearly every part of the world may have trouble using the sound correctly. Specifically:
- Speakers may turn [i] into the short sound [ɪ]. Thus, the word **deal** is mispronounced *dill*, and the word **seen** becomes *sin*.
- Other speakers may draw out the vowel when [i] comes before [l] The word **deal** is mispronounced as [diəl] or [di jəl]
    - o **Correction**: Keep the tongue high and tense in the mouth.

Contrast Pairs:

[i]	[ɪ]	[i]	[ɪ]
ease	is	feet	fit
leave	live	sleep	slip
cheap	chip	feel	fill
meal	mill	each	itch
gene	gin	scheme	skim
leased	list	beat	bit
seat	sit	sleet	slit
sheep	ship	reach	rich
seek	sick	peel	pill
seal	sill	seep	sip
keyed	kid	leafed	lift
heed	hid	steel	still

Words at Work:

Beginning	*Middle*	*Middle*
easel	extreme	marine
equipment	prescribe	receipt
either	meaning	protein
enough	steel	defense
equal	achievement	stream
evangelize	convenient	retrieve
eliminate	redeem	agreement
evening	teach	money
ether	repeat	field
east	complete	release
elongate	Japanese	speech
eager	presentation	decentralize

Practice Sentences for [i]

1. Steven completed the deal with his Taiwanese customer.
2. Each feature of the new system is easy to operate.
3. My departing manager gave an emotional speech to our team.
4. Marketing predicts a three percent increase in sales this week.
5. Even though we're behind schedule, we've caught many defects.
6. One key to success in the Philippines is attention to details.
7. The detection device caught someone sneaking into the building.
8. The population of Phoenix, Arizona, is increasing by leaps and bounds.
9. Maria had to choose between simultaneous speeches at the conference.
10. If we leave by three today we can get a cheap airfare to Costa Rica.
11. Please use the TV remote to decrease the volume and sharpen the screen.
12. We're delighted to host the beef industry leaders from Argentina.

♫ **Intonation**: Repeat the following phrases, some of which are American idioms. Emphasize the accented syllable to add rhythm and interest to your speech.

easy dóes it	on éasy street	leave it to mé
family trée	repeat after mé	new ecónomy
déal me in	field of dréams	Greek cuisíne
Louisiana chíli	delayed depárture	chéat sheet

[ɪ]

▶ **Lesson 20**

Sentence: Women have quickly risen to leadership positions in medicine, engineering and business.

Spelling Combinations for the sound [ɪ]

i as in **in**	**e** as in **England**	**o** as in **women**
u as in **business**	**ui** as in **quick**	**ei** as in **counterfeit**
ee as in **been**	**ie** as in **tier**	**y** as in **syrup**

Production: The sound [ɪ] is shorter in length than [i], so your lips and tongue are more relaxed. To make the sound, open your mouth slightly more than for [i]. Spread your lips, but don't smile. Arch the back of your tongue slightly lower and further back in the mouth than for [i] and place your tongue tip behind the lower front teeth.

Be Aware of These Problems with [ɪ]

- The sound [ɪ] is difficult for first language speakers of Spanish, Italian, French and Portuguese because the sound is not common in those languages. Speakers of Greek, Arabic and Hebrew also have trouble. When speakers see the letter *i* in a word, they usually substitute the long sound [i]. Thus, the word **simple** is incorrectly pronounced *seemple*, and the word **hit** becomes *heet.*
    - **Correction:** Keep the tongue lax and the lips less tense than for [i]. Listen for the distinction in the **Contrast Pairs** exercise below.
    - Realize that the letter *i* has several pronunciations in English.
- The sound [ɪ] is not hard to say, but sometimes speakers substitute the sound [ɛ]. Thus the word **pin** becomes *pen*, and the word **inside** is incorrectly pronounced *enside.*
    - **Correction:** Don't drop your jaw! Keep enough tension in the jaw to say [ɪ]. Listen closely to an American whose speech you admire.

Contrast Pairs:

[ɪ]	[i]	[ɪ]	[ɛ]
pit	Pete	pit	pet
rid	read	rid	red
sit	seat	sit	set
bid	bead	bid	bed
dill	deal	dill	dell
fill	feel	fill	fell
lid	lead	lid	led
rip	reap	rip	rep
hid	heed	hid	head
tin	teen	tin	ten
been	bean	bin	Ben
sill	seal	sill	sell

Words at Work:

Beginning	*Middle*	*Middle*
issue	validate	foreign
illustrate	architect	submit
initial	mistake	mystery
Italy	figure	build
institute	committee	system
impact	partition	heavily
incremental	shipped	priority
investigate	window	configuration
immediate	printer	situation
ignition	toxic	tariff
insulate	Manila	civil
irresponsible	peripheral	considerable

The [ɪɚ] Blend: The vowel [ɪ] is often combined with the sound [ɚ] to produce the diphthong [ɪɚ], as in the word ***here***. Note that the sound is different than for words ending in the letters **er**, as in diver. Keep your tongue tense for [ɪɚ].

Practice these common words you may hear at work:

appear	engineer	we're
career	clear	fearless
irregular	peer	gears
adhere	coherent	steer

Practice Sentences for the sound [ɪ]

1. The liquid in the cylinder turned to syrup.
2. Ilsa must adhere to a rigorous course of study for her new career.
3. Our initial settings for the instrument were inaccurate.
4. The Israeli engineer considered a digital solution for the bug.
5. The city building inspector approved the architect's plans.
6. It's difficult to fix the gears on a bicycle without good tools.
7. The Indian Ocean has more than six major shipping lanes.
8. The individual income tax rate is incredible.
9. Bill's administrative assistant had too much in her "in box."
10. If you're unwilling to appear ignorant, you can't learn.
11. The in-house newsletter printed our business mission and vision.
12. Jim filmed the office party on video and distributed it.

♫ **Intonation**: Repeat the following phrases, some of which are American idioms. Emphasize the accented syllable to add rhythm and interest to your voice.

English ídioms	windy Chicágo	itchy skín
dinner at síx	swíng shift	king of the híll
in the ínterim	India ínk	pícnic basket
inner cíty	insufficient íncome	italic prínting

[e] or [eɪ] ▶ Lesson 21

Sentence: The pl<u>a</u>ne was del<u>ay</u>ed <u>ei</u>ght hours, so I went to the airport caf<u>é</u> and <u>a</u>te a st<u>ea</u>k.

Spelling combinations for the sound [e]

a as in **plane**	**ay** as in **delay**	**ei** as in **eight**
e as in **cafe***	**ai** as in **train**	**et** as in **buffet***
au as in **gauge**	**ao** as in **chaos**	

* <u>Note</u>: The European endings ***é*** and ***et*** have been "Americanized" and are pronounced with a long sound [e].

Production: Place your tongue slightly lower than for the [ɪ] position. The back of your tongue should touch the upper back teeth, and the tip should be behind the lower front teeth. Relax your jaw and pull your lips back a little. Make a long sound.

Be Aware of these Problems with [e]

- This is a difficult sound for many speakers of Asian languages. Do not let your jaw drop or you will say [ɛ]. Speak slowly to produce the entire [e].
- Notice that the pure vowel [e] is lengthened into a diphthong [eɪ] when the sound comes before a voiced consonant. Thus: **state** [stet] vs. **stayed** [steɪd] and **grace** [gres] vs. **graze** [greɪz]
    - **Tip**: Hold the [e] longer if you tend to speak too quickly.

Contrast Pairs:

[e]	[ɛ]	[e]	[æ]
late	let	scrape	scrap
pain	pen	paced	past
wage	wedge	stake	stack
fail	fell	came	cam
sprayed	spread	taped	tapped
trade	tread	rain	ran
wailed	weld	Spain	span
taste	test	faced	fast
lanes	lens	take	tack
tale	tell	cased	cast
age	edge	pail	pal
date	debt	pace	pass

Words at Work:

Beginning	*Middle*	*End*
atypical	ratio	replay
Asia	maintenance	matinee
April	allocate	weigh
eight	breakage	Monday
aim	freight	resumé
able	Dane	relay
atrium	compilation	trade
agency	safety	convey
asymmetrical	sustain	fillet
aviation	escape	repay

Practice Sentences for [e]

1. Eight salespeople made their quota and celebrated with cake.
2. Saturday, April 8th, was rainy and cold.
3. Jane noticed the Danger! light and raced from her workstation.
4. Communication skills are a major consideration for a sales job.
5. If you have a backache, trade in your chair and table for new ones.
6. A replay of the game showed a chaotic second half.
7. The agency provided sustaining aid to hurricane victims.
8. Human Relations department reviewed my latest resumé.
9. We allocated the resources eight to one.
10. Bob met his Ukrainian friend in the atrium of the train station.
11. Please update James on the validation experiments.
12. A sign at the trade show reads, "If you break it, you pay for it."

♫ **Intonation**: Repeat the following phrases, some of which are American idioms. Emphasize the accented syllables to add rhythm and interest to your voice.

fréight train	great place to wórk	rélay race
trade relátions	belated hóliday	Asian vacátion
faithful ángel	eighth of an ácre	snáil mail
able to páy	ráilway station	háste makes wáste

[ɛ]

▶ **Lesson 22**

Sentence: My fr<u>ie</u>nd s<u>a</u>ys that <u>e</u>ducation is a way for <u>a</u>ny <u>e</u>mployee to <u>ge</u>t ah<u>ea</u>d in life.

Spelling Combinations for the sound [ɛ]

e as in **get**	**ea** as in **ahead**	**ai** as in **again**
a as in **says**	**ie** as in **friend**	**u** as in **bury**

Production: To pronounce [ɛ] open your mouth slightly wider than for [e]. Your tongue tip should rest behind the lower front teeth, and the back of the tongue should touch the upper molars. Your jaw drops slightly as you make the sound.

Be Aware of these Problems with [ɛ]

- Very few problems exist in producing this sound. Most languages have the sound, and it is commonly found in English words.
- Some speakers do, however, substitute either the sound [e] or [ɪ] for the sound [ɛ]. Instead of **pen**, they say *pain* or *pin*. As you do the **Contrast Pairs** exercise below, listen closely to the slight variations in sound. Adjust your tongue and jaw, so that the vowel sound corresponds to the word.

Contrast Pairs:

[ɛ]	[e]	[ɛ]	[ɪ]
set	sate	met	mitt
Mel	mail	set	sit
wet	wait	beg	big
sell	sale	wend	wind
let	late	lent	lint
sped	spade	pair	peer
debt	date	fleck	flick
well	whale	red	rid
bled	blade	spare	spear
tent	taint	etch	itch
bet	bait	hem	him
men	main	sled	slid

Words at Work:

Beginning	*Middle*	*Middle*
element	compelling	session
envelope	segment	adventure
execute	subsequent	process
extra	many	bench
entrance	strenuous	prestige
estimate	leather	never
energy	register	sector
exceed	intelligence	telephone
endeavor	consecutive	message
engineer	special	essential
experiment	recollect	penalty
engage	settings	contest

The Blend [ɛɚ]

The vowel [ɛ] is often combined with [ɚ] to produce the blend [ɛɚ], as in the word **software**. Watch for the spelling combinations ***ar*** or occasionally ***ear, air,*** or ***er*** for a clue as to when to pronounce this blend. Here are some practice words with [ɛɚ]:

careful	stairs	paradigm	spare	fare	share
prepare	territory	airline	error	character	chair

Practice Sentences for [ɛ]

1. Harry's sales territory covers most of Central America.
2. Please put the estimate in the envelope and send it to me.
3. We can ship the spare parts by airfreight the next day.
4. The weather in Paris can't be compared to that of Texas.
5. Dennis fell down the stairs and hit his head on a step.
6. Denmark sends us environment-friendly products.
7. Executing the strategy will require a pair of experts.
8. Every time there's an Elvis sighting, people forget their senses!
9. The marketing team pledges to enhance our web site.
10. We selected an eggshell paint color for the bedrooms.
11. Helen depends on her friends to help her with errands.
12. Jet engines can wear down without proper attention.

♫ **Intonation:** Repeat the following phrases, some of which are American idioms. Emphasize the accented syllable to add rhythm and interest to your voice.

end of an éra	economic incéntives	áirfare war
hárdware expert	essential élement	ecological impérative
pens and péncils	fresh lémons	wear and téar
West of Écuador	helpful emplóyee	cell phone connéction

Did she ask for a pin or a pen?

[æ]

► **Lesson 23**

Sentence: S<u>a</u>m l<u>au</u>ghed when P<u>a</u>trick fell fl<u>a</u>t on his b<u>a</u>ck.

Spelling combinations for [æ]

a as in **flat** **au** as in **laugh** **ai** as in **plaid**

Production: To make [æ] drop your jaw from the position for [ɛ]. Rest your tongue on the floor of your mouth, but keep it forward. Your tongue muscles should be relaxed.

Be Aware of these Problems with [æ]

- The sound [æ] is a characteristic American sound. It has regional differences within the U.S. Residents of New York, Boston, Chicago and states in the South all have a slightly different [æ] from the standard pronunciation.
- A problem for non-Americans, especially those who speak British English, is substituting [ɑ] for [æ]. Thus the word **class** [klæs] becomes [klɑs].
- Americans enjoy listening to British English, but if your native accent is layered over a British accent, you run the risk of not being understood.
    - **Correction**: If you've spent a lifetime saying [ɑ] in place of [æ], concentrate on dropping your jaw and keeping your tongue ***forward*** and on the bottom of the mouth.

Contrast Pairs:

[æ]	[ɑ]	[æ]	[ɑ]
batch	botch	ramp	romp
racket	rocket	pad	pod
band	bond	backs	box
shack	shock	lab	lob
laughed	loft	add	odd
clack	clock	mask	mosque
jab	job	nab	knob
lap	lop	smack	smock
chap	chop	lack	lock
rack	rock	fax	fox
lag	log	plaid	plod
bang	bong	flap	flop

Words at Work:

Beginning	*Middle*	*Middle*
analyze	standard	classify
amplify	backspace	language
anticipate	massive	status
activate	malleable	damage
advisory	bandwidth	random
atom	hammer	casualty
antenna	plant	backbone
angle	hazard	cancel
anchor	brand	practice
adamant	panel	passport
attitude	factory	chapter
answer	stack	intact

Practice Sentences for the sound [æ]

1. My world atlas was valuable when I traveled to Antarctica.
2. Thanks for the gigantic anniversary banner.
3. Dan eats an apple every afternoon after lunch.
4. My manager has a map of Alabama on his wall.
5. We must give those alloyed parts an acid bath.
6. A fascinating aspect of the issue is bandwidth.
7. Angry animals from the Amazon attacked our car.
8. Tan handled the allocation demands adequately.
9. There's a mismatch between our plans and our actions.
10. This standard application form has a lot of blanks.
11. I danced the tango at my anniversary party.
12. My laptop can write in Spanish and Italian.

♫ **Intonation**: Repeat the following phrases, some of which are American idioms. Emphasize the accented syllable to add rhythm and interest to your voice.

lánd mass	handheld scánner	candid cámera
backward slásh	down to brass tácks	plan of attáck
áction plan	Grand Ávenue	hatch a plán
Stand báck!	after the fáct	a bad hábit

Word Wise: Note words that you mispronounced or hesitated to say. Write down the phonetic pronunciation and/or stress mark for future reference.

__________ __________ __________ __________ __________
__________ __________ __________ __________ __________
__________ __________ __________ __________ __________
__________ __________ __________ __________ __________

↓

Contractions: You can or you can't?

Americans use contracted verb forms [called contractions] all the time when speaking. Contractions are informal, so while they're acceptable in speech, written narrative and email messages, they're not used when writing reports or other formal documents. This book uses contractions because its goal is to teach you how to *speak* English.

Miscommunication can occur when using contractions if the ending sound is not clear. There's a 180° difference between can and can't.

While you don't have to use contractions, and in fact shouldn't if you feel you will be misunderstood, contractions are an essential element to an American speech rhythm. As you master the language, you'll want to use contractions.

Practice these commonly used contractions:

Affirmative		*Negative*	
I am	I'm	is not	isn't
you are	you're	are not	aren't
he is	he's	was not	wasn't
she is	she's	were not	weren't
it is	it's	do not	don't
we are	we're	does not	doesn't
they are	they're	did not	didn't
I will	I'll	will not	won't
you will	you'll	have not	haven't
she will	she'll	has not	hasn't
etc.		cannot	can't
I have	I've	could not	couldn't
you have	you've	should not	shouldn't
we have	we've	must not	mustn't
etc.			
that is	that's		
there is	there's		
what is	what's		
I would	I'd		
you had	you'd		
they had	they'd		
we would	we'd		

Review: The Front Vowels

Read across a line. Be careful to distinguish the vowel sounds.

[i]	[ɪ]	[e]	[ɛ]	[æ]
bead	bid	bade	bed	bad
deed	did	Dade	dead	dad
neat	knit	innate	net	gnat
lead	lid	laid	led	lad
keen	kin	cane	Ken	can
meet	mitt	mate	met	mat
heel	hill	hail	hell	Hal
beat	bit	bait	bet	bat
seat	sit	sate	set	sat
seal	sill	sale	sell	Sal
peen	pin	pain	pen	pan
seeks	six	sakes	sex	sacks

"e frɛnd ɪn nid ɪs a frɛnd ɪndid."

~ Proverb

►◄ **Dialogue**: Practice the following dialogue. Remember to use intonation and stress in order to give your voice more interest and your words more meaning. The dialogue contains American idioms and informal speech patterns.

The Offsite Team Meeting

Manager: Welcome to the offsite. It's a first for our team.

David: I see that the agenda includes a discussion of our three-year plan.

William: Thank goodness. The strategic plan needs revision.

Chen: Yes, the market has changed so quickly.

Pat: The data shows that sales in three key regions are off by twenty percent.

Debbie: So we've got to rethink our product mix.

Cindy: Maybe, but a knee jerk reaction to one quarterly sales report is dangerous.

David: Agreed.

Venkat: Let's be clear where we're headed with this discussion.

Debbie: Are we talking long-term strategy?

Cindy: Or simply issues around this recent sales data?

Chen: As far as I can see, they deserve equal attention.

Manager: Then let's begin with an analysis of Pat's data.

Chapter Eight
Back Vowels

[ɑ, ɔ, o, ʊ, u]

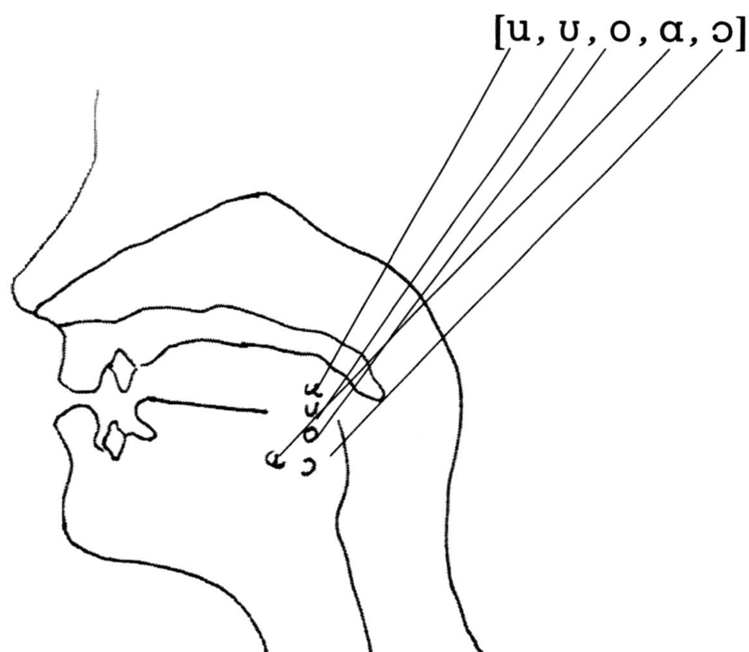

Back vowels are formed by movement of the back of the tongue in relation to the soft palate. Rounded lips are important in all but one of the sounds.

[ɑ - ɔ]

► **Lesson 24**

Sentence: [ɑ] S<u>o</u>rry, I didn't have kn<u>ow</u>ledge of the al<u>a</u>rm on the l<u>o</u>ck.

Sentence: [ɔ] He b<u>ough</u>t a fl<u>aw</u>ed yet c<u>o</u>stly desk at the F<u>a</u>ll <u>au</u>ction.

Spelling Combinations for the sound [ɑ]

o as in **sorry** **ow** as in **knowledge** **a** as in **al<u>a</u>rm**
ea as in **heart**

Spelling Combinations for the sound [ɔ]

aw as in **flawed** **o** as in **often** **au** as in **auction**
ough as in **bought** **augh** as in **taught** **a** as in **fall**

Production: The mouth position for [ɑ] is the widest of any of the vowels. To make the sound, open your mouth and say ***aaaah***, as though you were responding to your doctor's request.

To say [ɔ] close the mouth a little from the position of [æ] and round your lips slightly. Raise the back of your tongue a bit but don't touch your upper teeth.

<u>Note</u>: Pronunciation of both [ɑ] and [ɔ] varies from region to region, even word to word, within the U.S. In many cases native speakers don't even make a distinction between the two sounds. Thus, pronouncing the subtle difference between [ɑ] and [ɔ] is less important than that ***you distinguish* [ɑ/ɔ] *from* [o] *or* [ə/ʌ], *which are definitely different sounds.*

Be Aware of these Problems with [ɑ]

- While [ɑ] is easy to produce, many languages do not use this exact sound, so it becomes hard to identify in English words, particularly when combined with the letter ***o,*** which is mispronounced closer to [o] than correctly as [ɑ].

  Examples: The words **hot, often, box, lock** have the letter ***o*** but take [ɑ].
  - **Correction**: Keep your jaw very relaxed and your mouth wide. Do not round your lips at all. Pay close attention to native speakers, and note that when you see the letter ***o*** in a word, it might be pronounced as [ɑ]. You'll have to memorize some words because there's no rule in English that will tell you when the ***o*** is pronounced [o] or [ɑ].
- The sound [ɔ] is mispronounced when the lips are rounded too much. Thus, the word **law** [lɔ] is mispronounced as *læw*.
  - **Correction**: Keep your lips only slightly rounded. Don't make a [w] sound.

Comparison:

[ɑ]	[ɔ]	[ɑ]	[ɔ]
hock	hawk	wok	walk
sod	sawed	pond	pawned
odd	awed	stock	stalk
bobble	bauble	cot	caught
holler	hauler	collar	caller
tock	talk	tot	taught

Contrast Pairs:

[ɑ]	[o]	[ɑ]	[ʌ]
cot	coat	cot	cut
not	note	fond	fund
doll	dole	lock	luck
stock	stoke	dock	duck
sock	soak	bog	bug
hop	hope	model	muddle
ox	oaks	rob	rub
pop	pope	gosh	gush
pock	poke	hog	hug
calm	comb	stomp	stump
bond	boned	jot	jut
Tom	tome	shot	shut

Words at Work:	*Beginning*	*Middle*	*Middle*
[ɑ]	occupy	modern	follow
	operations	probably	clock
	honest	respond	prompt
	onsite	economics	swap
	obsolete	accommodate	heartland
	obvious	watchdog	solve
	optimal	complex	stoppage
	obtain	slot	contract
	oxygen	hardware	locker
	opportunity	beyond	concentration
	oscillate	politics	wattage
	observe	cardboard box	block

The blend [ɑɚ]

The sound [ɑ] is often combined with [ɚ] to form the blend [ɑɚ], as in the word **article.** You'll find this sound in the spelling combination ***ar*** or ***uar***. Here are a few practice words:

art	architect	smart	guard	target	army
car	alarm	card	parts	larger	argue

Practice Sentences for [ɑ]

1. The dot.com economy won't make other businesses obsolete.
2. My alarm clock warns me to head off for my job.
3. Our parts are docked in the harbor at Abu Dhabi.
4. Don often swaps stories with friends in his department.
5. Palm trees line some city blocks in Los Angeles.
6. The startup firm developed a smart, new kind of lock.
7. Argentina has a strong market in beef products.
8. If you spot a frog on the road, return it to the pond.
9. Bob and Tom attended the conference in the Bahamas.
10. I jotted down the message I spotted on the kiosk.
11. Ottawa is located in the province of Ontario.
12. "Stop!" yelled the armed guard as onlookers watched.

♫ **Intonation:** Repeat the following phrases, some of which are American idioms. Emphasize the accented syllable to add rhythm and interest.

óbvious opportúnity	on my hónor	on the wáterfront
optic technólogy	artful dódger	cóntract emplóyee
ponder the próblem	on a lárk	hot chócolate
artifícial héart	hót spot	heart to héart

Words at Work [ɔ]	*Beginning*	*Middle*	*End*
	audit	cause	law
	awkward	long-term	draw
	often	broad	flaw
	August	fought	raw
	audio	launch	straw
	alternative	install	paw
	author	applause	gnaw
	awesome	wrong	thaw
	always	prong	saw
	offer	cough	craw
	audition	coffee	maw
	awning	thought	slaw

Note: In some regions of the U.S., the letters ***or*** form a blend [ɔɚ]. **Examples: order, core**. Most Americans simply say [oɚ], which is the preferred pronunciation in this book. Listen to the pronunciation of Americans that you meet.

Practice Sentences for the sounds [ɑ] and [ɔ]

1. Connie ordered almond toffee with her hot milk.
2. On the line we always wear safety goggles.
3. The shop foreman applauded his team's efforts.
4. The Austrian Alps are an awesome sight.
5. At the auction I bought a wok and a chopping block.
6. Audrey drinks a lot of coffee but not any soda pop.
7. The auditors found the root cause of the problem.
8. Austin, Texas, experienced an awesome autumn.
9. Don gets claustrophobia in his small cubicle.
10. The sawmill reported a loss for the fourth quarter.
11. John swam to shore using the Australian crawl.
12. The attorney-at-law said our contract was solid.

[o] or [oʊ] ▶ Lesson 25

Sentence: I'll thr<u>ow</u> out a r<u>o</u>pe even th<u>ough</u> the b<u>oa</u>t has sunk.

Spelling combinations for the sound [o]

o as in **rope** **ow** as in **throw** **ough** as in **though**
oa as in **boat** **oe** as in **toe**

Production: Round and protrude your lips, and raise your jaw to a higher position than for [ɑ]. Raise the back of your tongue mid-high, and point the tip behind the lower teeth.

Be Aware of these Problems with [o]

- Spanish speakers, and those from the Mediterranean and North and Central Africa, often do not pronounce a true [o]. Rather, the sound is somewhere between [o] and [ɑ] – a sound we don't have in English. It's important to develop a long [o] sound.
- When the [o] is stressed or is followed by a voiced sound, it often becomes a blend [oʊ]. **Examples: note – node coat – code**. This blend distinction isn't a major issue, nor is it problematic except for speakers who talk so fast that they "clip" the blended sound, and are therefore misunderstood. Speakers from India and Pakistan are likely to clip the sound. Slow down!

Contrast Pairs:

[o]	[ɑ/ɔ]	[o]	[ɑʊ]
coat	cot	hose	house
boat	bought	bow	bow
so	saw	honed	hound
note	not	roast	roust
code	cod	sew	sow
poke	pock	a load	aloud
lope	lop	tone	town
wrote	rot	coach	couch
cope	cop	goat	gout
soak	sock	known	noun
smoke	smock	moaned	mound
rote	rot	dose	douse

Words at Work:

Beginning	*Middle*	*End*
order	probe	video
organize	portable	window
overview	priority	zero
omit	console	follow
overseas	keystroke	dough
oriental	motivate	cash flow
opinion	roadmap	although
omega	local	ego
ocean	control	fellow
ownership	platform	grow
only	toner	portfolio
ohm	oppose	ditto

Practice Sentences for [o]

1. The exported stoves are on a slow boat to Indonesia.
2. The Rolling Stones attract enormous audiences worldwide.
3. We were not impressed by the vendor's dog and pony show.
4. Our hotel in Portland, Oregon, was one of the best.
5. Antonio felt as if he were on overload, so he phoned for help.
6. Joe found an online course in automotive engineering.
7. Please control your robot before he goes wild.
8. We rode over old roads to an oasis in Oman.
9. We came in from the cold snow and toasted our toes by the fire.
10. The service provider hosts lots of O'Brien domain names.
11. Our mode of coping with hunger is to order tacos.
12. The bolt will soon be obsolete, so we must find another source.

♫ **Intonation**: Repeat the following phrases, some of which are American idioms. Emphasize the accented syllable to add rhythm and interest.

cold shóulder
hold your hórses
Phone hóme!
stone cóld

open enróllment
órgan donor
don't throw stónes
hope and glóry

know the rópes
room and bóard
roly-póly
oceangoing bóat

[ʊ - u]

▶ Lesson 26

Sentence: **[ʊ]** If I could make cookies without sugar. I would.

Spelling Combinations for the sound [ʊ]

ou as in **could/would** **oo** as in **cook**ies **u** as in **sugar**

Production: To make [ʊ], relax the lips, drop your tongue slightly and let the sound come from the back of the throat.

Sentence: **[u]** Who in the newsroom can cover the story of the cruise ship that crashed on the sand dune?

Spelling Combinations for the sound [u]

o as in **who** **ew** as in **news** **oo** as in **room**
ui as in **cruise** **ou** as in **you** **u** as in **dune**
oe as in **shoe** **ue** as in **clue**

Production: To make [u], round your lips noticeably so that there is only a small opening. Raise the back of your tongue to where it almost touches the soft palate. Your tongue tip should be just behind your front teeth as you produce voice.

Be Aware of these Problems with [ʊ] and [u]

- The sounds [ʊ] nor [u] are seldom misarticulated, but speakers are often confused as to when to use [ʊ] and when to use [u]. The **Contrast Pairs** exercise below will help you distinguish the two sounds. Unfortunately, as with all English vowels, you can't always tell the pronunciation by the spelling. You will have to memorize some words.
- [ʊ] is sometimes combined with the sound [ɚ] make the sound [ʊɚ]. Try the following words that have the [ʊɚ] blend:
  poor endure ensure tourist you're

Contrast Pairs

[u]	[ʊ]	[u]	[o]	[ʊ]	[ʌ]
suit	soot	crew	crow	look	luck
fool	full	glue	glow	put	putt
pool	pull	shoe	show	took	tuck
stewed	stood	knew	know	book	buck
who'd	hood	whose	hose	stood	stud
Luke	look	ooze	Os	hoof	huff
gooey	goody	root	wrote	could	cud
kooky	cookie	ghoul	goal	rook	ruck
nuke	nook	blue	blow	shook	shuck

Words at Work:

[u]	[u]	[ju]	[ʊ]
remove	plume	unit	bulletin
rules	prod<u>u</u>ce	fuel	undertook
root	school	universal	mistook
toolbox	include	fuse	should
loose	through	document	push
proof	ensure	utility	goods
tutor	Tuesday*	overview	shook
assume	boot	user	couldn't
overdue	threw	module	livelihood
room	true	menu	pulley
include	boom	values	hook
news*	illuminate	union	sugary

*The vowel in these words is occasionally pronounced [ju].

♫ **Intonation:** Repeat the following phrases, some of which are American idioms. Emphasize the accented syllables to add rhythm and interest.

flew the cóop	overdue bóoks	true to my róots
tóothpaste tube	rúle book	by hóok or by cróok
blooming túlips	new ménu	Cuban músic
wooden shóes	shook the bróom	boot it úp

Practice Sentences for [u] and [ʊ]

1. Plumes of steam rose from the flue at the soup factory.
2. The crew produced a good batch of cookies on Tuesday.
3. Our tour book explains how to drive in Kuala Lumpur.
4. The root cause is a loose screw on the pulley.
5. Scientists know that the proof is in the pudding.
6. Kids in school say that Joel is a cool dude.
7. Julia assumed ownership of the new tool.
8. When cruising through New Mexico, obey the rules of the road.
9. Luckily, he fell from the roof onto a cushion and had a good laugh.
10. An old Hindu custom calls for a ritual at noon.
11. Stewart stood up to the bully at school and pushed him away.

▣ **Idea for a Conversation**: "**Hooked on a Book**"

Discuss a book that's been important to you. Perhaps it's on your shelf at home or at work. It may be a book you remember from childhood. It might be a scientific, business, religious, historical, reference, travel, or cookbook, or even a novel that tells a story you'll never forget.

Word Wise: Note words that you mispronounced or hesitated to say. Write down the phonetic spelling and/or add a stress mark for future reference.

__________ __________ __________ __________ __________

__________ __________ __________ __________ __________

__________ __________ __________ __________ __________

↓

►◄**Dialogue:** Practice the following dialogue. In addition to numerous words containing the sounds from this chapter, you'll encounter American idioms and informal words and phrases.

Retail

Clerk: Could I show you the new suits from Hong Kong?

Lou: I don't wear suits to work. We're very casual at my company.

Clerk: True, people think they need a suit only for a funeral.

Lou: However, I do have a job interview coming up soon.

Clerk: It always looks good to wear a stylish suit.

Lou: All right, help me choose a suit. Not too expensive, though.

Clerk: This one's casual and yet suitable for any situation.

Lou: Good. I wear a suit once in a blue moon, so it needs to be versatile.

[Lou returns after trying it on]

Lou: It's a little loose through the shoulders.

Clerk: No problem. We can alter it by tomorrow. Would that work?

Lou: Yes, my interview is on Tuesday. Could you deliver it to me?

Clerk: Of course. And now, we must do something about those blue boots you're wearing!

Chapter Nine
The Middle Vowels

[ʌ ə] [ɝ ɚ]

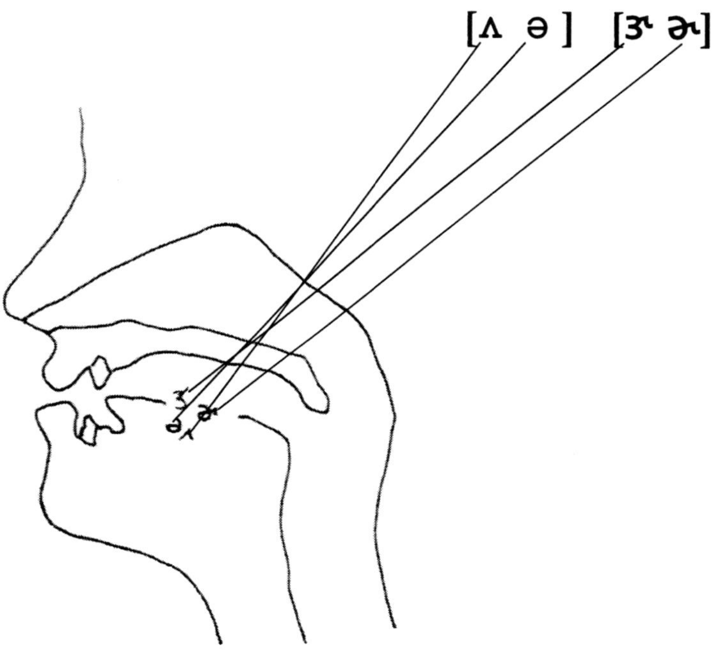

Syllable stress within words is critical to determining the production of the two sets of middle vowels. The middle vowel sounds [ʌ] and [ɝ] are pronounced in stressed syllables. When the sounds appear in unstressed syllables within words, the slightly different sounds [ə] and [ɚ] are produced.

[ʌ – ə] ▶ Lesson 27

Sentence [ʌ]: The troubling update from my uncle came a month late.

Spelling combinations for the *stressed* sound [ʌ]

u as in **up** **ou** as in **trouble** **o** as in **month**
oe as in **does** **oo** as in **flood**

Sentence [ə]: The Stevens family traveled across Canada with their cameras and their pet cobra.

Spelling combinations for the unstressed sound [ə]

a, e, i, o, u, and any vowel combination that appears in an unstressed syllable in a word can be sounded as [ə].

Production: To say [ʌ], open your mouth and relax your jaw and tongue. Raise the central part of your tongue slightly, but don't round your lips. Produce voice.

The unstressed vowel [ə] is formed in the same way, but the sound is shorter and weaker.

The Schwa [ə]

The unstressed sound [ə] is the most common sound in the English language. That is because other vowels often change from their original sound to [ə] when they are unstressed.

Example: The letter ***a*** [e] becomes the sound [ə] in the words **again** [əgɛn] or **banana** [bənænə].

The [ə] sound is so common that it has its own name, **schwa** [ʃwɑ], which comes from a German word that means "weak."

Note that the word **the** is pronounced [ðə] when it precedes a word beginning with a consonant. Examples: **the** desk, **the** key, **the** pen.

Be Aware of these Problems with [ʌ] and [ə]

- The [ʌ/ə] sound does not exist in many languages, so non-native speakers of English often substitute [ɑ] or another sound. Thus, instead of correctly pronouncing the word **luck** [lʌk], they may say [lɑk] – which is misunderstood as *lock*.
  - **Correction**: Do not "over pronounce" the sound. Keep your tongue relaxed. If someone does not understand you, consider that your problem might be too much vowel sound.
- Because the unstressed schwa [ə] occurs in so many spelling combinations, it may be difficult for you to know when to use it.
  - **Tip**: Listen to Americans as they speak at work, on the radio or on TV. Write down familiar words and place the schwa symbol [ə] above the vowel to remind yourself of the pronunciation.
  - Your dictionary can be very useful in identifying which vowels are pronounced as [ə].

Contrast Pairs:

[ʌ]	[ɑ]	[ʌ]	[ɑ]
shut	shot	nut	not
bug	bog	cluck	clock
luck	lock	one	wan
sputter	spotter	cut	cot
stuck	stock	rubber	robber
fund	fond	shuck	shock
nuzzle	nozzle	jug	jog
flux	flocks	lull	loll
pump	pomp	tug	tog
come	calm	muddle	model
smug	smog	slush	slosh
duck	dock	rut	rot

Words at Work [ʌ]:

double	update	customer	function
ultimate	brush	enough	instruct
oven	upright	ultra	multiple
under	rubble	suburb	shutter
London	discuss	stunned	subsequent
comfort	upward	suddenly	public

Words at Work [ə]:

Beginning	*Middle*	*Middle/End*
approach	machinery	warranty
agenda	current	benefit
attempt	channel	possible
afford	capable	atom
oppose	method	option
assumption	dialogue	idea
agreement	implement	dilemma
apology	electrical	visa
arrangement	dictionary	Asia
appreciate	experiment	antenna
appropriate	annual	efficient
amend	technical	hundred

Practice Sentences for [ʌ] and [ə]

1. Gina complied with the shut off request from her manager.
2. Our amazing product is the best thing under the sun.
3. Don't eat too much junk food or you'll get an upset tummy.
4. The dense fog in London comes in certain months of the year.
5. What an ugly duckling! Only a mother could love such a thing!
6. Instruction on the new computer started in August.
7. Undelivered supplies of duct tape are stuck at the dock at Customs.
8. An abrupt change in the market caused us to ramp up production.
9. Nutty peanut butter is the favorite snack food in Atlanta.
10. The conference in Canada attracted numerous attendees.
11. Air conditioning is standard in upscale rental cars.
12. The savannah in Kenya is home to zebras and lions.

♫ **Intonation**: Repeat the following phrases, some of which are American idioms. Emphasize the accented syllable to add rhythm and interest to your voice.

stuck in a rút	cut the ápron strings	double úp
mission contról	under discússion	Idaho spúd
come undóne	cómfort zone	áir duct
rubber dúck	on crútches	banana splít
cover úp	[note the different meaning]	cóver up

[ɝ – ɚ]

► **Lesson 28**

Sentence [ɝ]: An urgent call from an attorney made her nervous early in the morning.

Spelling Combinations for the sound [ɝ]

er as in **her**	**ear** in in **early**	**ur** as in **urgent**
or as in **attorney**	**ir** as in **first**	**our** as in **journey**

Sentence [ɚ]: My manager pointed out the error in the supplier's data.

Spelling Combinations for [ɚ]

Any vowel and **r** combination in the unstressed position can produce the sound [ɚ].

Production: To produce [ɝ] open your mouth halfway and don't round your lips. Raise the middle of your tongue slightly and curl the tip back until it points to the palate just behind the upper gum ridge.

[ɚ] is produced in the same way, but don't say the sound as loudly, and don't hold it as long as for [ɝ].

Be Aware of these Problems with [ɝ] and [ɚ]

- Speakers whose native language is Spanish or one of the other Latin-based languages often substitute [ɛɚ] in place of [ɝ] or [ɚ]. Thus, the word **her** is incorrectly pronounced *hair* [hɛɚ]. This mispronunciation occurs quite frequently and causes the listener to be confused.
    - **Correction**: Tense your tongue as you curl it back, and round your lips slightly. Be aware that when you see words spelled with ***ear***, ***er***, ***or***, etc., you'll need to be conscious of the correct pronunciation.
- Make sure to pronounce the proper sound [ɚ], and not invert it to an incorrect [rə] pronunciation. Thus, the word perform is *pɚform*, not the incorrect [priform].

Words at Work [ɝ]:

	Beginning	*Middle*	*Middle*
	earnest	learn	curve
	early	perfect [adj]	thorough
	earth	personal	purchase
	urge	version	birthday
	earnings	alert	virtual
	urgent	purpose	third
	urban	quirk	determine
Middle	per	heard	absurd
	current	reserve	Thursday
	merge	concern	firm
	thirst	courage	world
	hurdle	term	service

Words at Work [ɚ]:

Middle	*Middle*	*End*
perhaps	overview	picture
forward	authorize	processor
modern	opportunity	dollar
percent	confirmation	figure
Internet	outward	broker
western	standard	feature
preference	auxiliary	recorder
conservation	parameter	solar
repercussion	surprise	manager
leverage	government	sector
interstate	underwrite	flier

Practice Sentences for [ɝ] and [ɚ]

1. The courteous taxi driver delivered his rider to the hotel curb.
2. Switzerland confirmed it would forward payment in dollars.
3. We were nervous as we observed the turtle cross Interstate 5.
4. Bernie noticed furniture disappearing from the room.
5. The early bird catches the worm.
6. Never operate a coffee grinder while herding cows.
7. Higher education should ensure you greater earning power.
8. The sensors alerted us to the burning component.
9. Be sure to enter the lottery and win a trip to Germany.
10. If we hurry we'll get the furnace fixed in just over an hour.
11. The merchandise from our supplier comes in popular colors.
12. Current procedures permit us to import bird feeders.

♫ **Intonation**: Repeat the following phrases, some of which contain American idioms. Emphasize the accented syllable for rhythm and interest.

fénder bender	under the wéather	círcuit breaker
sérvice provider	iron cúrtain	úrban center
perfect círcle	mother náture	workahólic
charitable dónor	search and recóvery	blur of cólor

▣ Idea for a Conversation: "Customer Service"

Your organization likely provides a product or a service to customers, most of whom you never meet. But in life we're all customers. Recall and discuss a time when you were a customer and received excellent or terrible customer service.

Shift of Accent
Common Words at Work

Words spelled identically may be accented differently, depending on their use in the sentence. Following is a list of common words. You need to know the context of how the word is used in order to determine the stress. **Note the pattern: the first syllable of a noun is stressed, while the second syllable of a verb is stressed. Adjectives vary but usually follow the noun stress.**

Noun	***Verb***	***Adjective***
récord	recórd	récord [store]
próduce	prodúce	
óbject	objéct	
súrvey	survéy	súrvey [team]
pérmit	permít	
cónduct	condúct	
présent	presént	
	perféct	pérfect [day]
cónvert	convért	
réplay	repláy	
súspect	suspéct	
récall	recáll	
ínvalid		inválid [data]
súbject	subjéct	

◙ **Practice Exercise**: Choose a pair of words from the box above and use them in a statement. Stress the two words correctly.

Example: I recáll the newspaper story of the defective part récall.

Speak Effectively at Work

Break the "er……uh…." Habit

Whether you're speaking one-on-one with a coworker or giving a presentation in front of a group, you want your speech to be crisp, lively and authoritative.

The filler sounds "er" and "uh" deaden your voice and make your message much less effective. All the work you've done to improve your pronunciation and intonation will be minimized unless you rid your speech of these counterproductive sounds.

Speakers may believe that such sounds "fill the silence" and provide time to think of what to say next. In reality, most speakers are simply afraid of pausing between thoughts. They think they must "fill the gap." Do not be afraid of silence. ***A pause to reflect on a question or to give the listener time to absorb your message can be very effective.***

Furthermore, if your accent in English is strong, you will want to give listeners time to adjust to your accent or rhythm. Those fillers may prevent the listener from "tuning in" to your accent.

Many native American English speakers are also guilty of using fillers. In addition to "*er*" and "*uh*", you'll hear these fillers: "*okay?*" "*you know*" "*right*", as well as "*and*" between every phrase, so that a sentence is never completed.

Tips to Eliminate Fillers:

✓ Record your speech on audio or video. Really hear yourself in order to determine which fillers you use. Become aware of your speech habits.

✓ Practice coming to a complete stop after a thought. Glide your voice down at the end of a sentence. Hold the silence a half second.

✓ Realize that a short pause is truly shorter than you think.

✓ Ask a friend or coworker to point out your "fillers" habit to you.

►◄ Dialogue: Practice the following dialogue. In addition to numerous words containing the sounds from this chapter, you'll encounter American idioms and informal speech patterns.

A Potential New Customer

Seller: The current *Funeller** comes with features to help you cater to all your customers.

Buyer: But once our company expands into Canada, can you serve us?

Seller: Of course. Our service support extends throughout North America.

Buyer: How do we keep current on new options?

Seller: Early update notifications. Plus quarterly service bulletins.

Buyer: I'm interested, but I need to think it over.

Seller: Sure, I understand. But if you purchase now, I'm authorized to offer a thirty percent discount.

Buyer: What about purchase terms?

Seller: We can surely work out credit. And include a monthly service contract.

Buyer: Fine. But I need to run the idea by my partner. Her input is critical.

Seller: Could I stop by later this afternoon to show her the *Funeller*?

Buyer: Monday is better. She's in a conference with a supplier, and I'm overwhelmed with work.

Seller: How about Monday at eleven? I'll come with my best offer.

* *Fictitious product*

Chapter Ten
The Blends
[Diphthongs]

[ɑɪ ɑʊ ɔɪ]

Diphthongs are blended vowel sounds made by gliding the tongue continuously from the position for one vowel to that of another within the same syllable. The stress is on the first part of the blended sound.

[ɑɪ] ▶ **Lesson 29**

Sentence: Simon decided to buy the bright diamond when he saw the look in his wife's eyes.

Spelling Combinations for the sound [ɑɪ]

i as in **wife** **uy** as in **buy** **igh** as in **bright** **y** as in **try**
ie as in **tie** **ei** as in **height** **ai** as in **aisle** **ey** as in **eye**
ui as in **guide** **ia** as in **diamond** **ye** as in **dye**

Production: Open your mouth as if to say [ɑ]. Keep your tongue flat and relaxed on the bottom of your mouth. Don't round your lips. As you produce voice, glide the back of your tongue toward the position of [ɪ]. You want more tongue movement than jaw movement. Your jaw moves only very slightly straight up.

Be Aware of these Problems with [ɑɪ]

- Many speakers from Asia fail to produce the entire sound. Thus, they produce only half of the sound [ɑ], instead of the entire sound, [ɑɪ]. **Example**: the word **time** [tɑɪm] is mispronounced as *tahm* [tɑm].
    - **Correction**: Keep your tongue relaxed. Too much tension in the back of your tongue causes this problem.
- Speakers whose first language is Spanish or another of the Latin-based languages see the *letter **i*** and pronounce it as they would do in their native tongue: ***ee*** [i] Thus the word **vine** [vɑɪn] is mispronounced *veen* [vin].
    - **Correction**: Recognize that the letter ***i*** in English may be pronounced [ɑɪ], but that ***i*** has several pronunciations. You'll want to expand your speaking vocabulary by memorizing some words.

Contrast Pairs:

[ɑɪ]	[i]	[ɑɪ]	[ɪ]
file	feel	fine	fin
sign	seen	bind	binned
flight	fleet	gripe	grip
time	team	height	hit
eyes	ease	dime	dim
dial	deal	tile	till
height	heat	heist	hissed
pile	peel	kite	kit
site	seat	time	Tim
grind	greened	might	mitt
style	steel	I'll	ill
vial	veal	bite	bit

Words at Work:

Beginning/Middle	*Middle*	*Middle/End*
itemize	guideline	try
idea	pliers	apply
aisle	priority	refine
isobar	reconcile	design
ironed	flashlight	coincide
isometric	archive	buy
iodine	scientific	comply
minus	wise	fly
decline	require	guy
isotope	utilize	high
icon	finite	price
certified	ninety-nine	rely

Practice Sentences for [ɑɪ]

1. Kyle rode his bike all the way around Ireland.
2. I informed the team of our ideal time frame for closure.
3. In Iowa the corn grows sky high.
4. I tied down the file cabinet so it wouldn't slide away.
5. The tool on aisle five requires a final check.
6. Lila said I'd need pliers and a hammer on the line.
7. Please say goodbye quietly because my child is asleep.
8. I do isometric exercises on long flights to Cairo.
9. A virus in our computers idled nine employees.
10. Ivan provided the archive library with data on isotopes.
11. We rely on the guys from R&D for good ideas.
12. You must itemize your statements to reconcile the accounts.

♫ **Intonation**: Repeat the following phrases, some of which are American idioms. Emphasize the accented syllable for rhythm and interest.

high priórity	fíght or flíght	bright idéa
high and drý	the time of your lífe	wide awáke
a white líe	lífe is príceless	eyes on the príze
high-mínded	Irish éyes	dry íce

Do you "ice" "ise" or "ize" it?

A confusing aspect of English pronunciation concerns these three endings. Each has the letter ***i*** [ɑɪ], followed by the letters ***ce, se***, or ***ze***. Here's a general guideline for pronouncing words with these spellings. Note that the stress falls on the syllable with [ɑɪ].

Noun [ɑɪs]	**Verb [ɑɪz]**	**Verb [ɑɪz]**
device	to devise	–
advice	to advise	–
–	–	to mobilize
–	–	to initialize
–	–	to prioritize
–	–	to modernize

[ɑʊ] ▶ **Lesson 30**

Sentence: The cr<u>ow</u>d ran for high gr<u>ou</u>nd when the water rose.

Spelling Combinations for the sound [ɑʊ]

ou as in **ground** **ow** as in **crowd**

Production: Open your mouth as if to say [ɑ]. Keep your tongue relaxed and flat. Then, as you produce voice, close and round your lips and raise your tongue a little.

Be Aware of these Problems with [ɑʊ]

- This sound is not difficult to produce. However, when it is in combination with the sound [n], many Asian language speakers fail to say the [n]. Thus, the word **round** [rɑʊnd] is mispronounced *roud* [rɑʊd]. Remember to say the [n]. You may want to turn to the section on [n] for more practice.
- Some speakers substitute [o] for [ɑʊ].
    - **Correction:** Keep your tongue flat and as you begin do not round your lips. Only round them a little at the end of the sound.

Contrast Pairs:

[ɑʊ]	[o] or [oʊ]
bound	boned
found	phoned
now	know
couch	coach
towel	toll
mound	moaned
hour	oar
crowd	crowed
aloud	a load
out	oat
sound	sewn
how	hoe
town	tone

Words at Work: *All Positions*

crowded	hourly
doubt	outline
announce	pound
aloud	scout
county	download
tower	allowance
south	oust
crown	pronounce
about	gown
outdoors	ounce
brown	ourselves
mount	astound

Practice Sentences for [ɑʊ]

1. Howard announced that he needed a clean towel.
2. We found several usable chairs piled outdoors in the rain.
3. Townhouses sell for a premium price in this county.
4. Reading aloud can help you pronounce words correctly.
5. Mount the bracket a foot down from the ceiling.
6. South Korea is becoming a powerful trading partner.
7. The crowd ousted the outlaw from the town square.
8. I doubt we can finish the project in an hour.
9. The Puget Sound area is home to a crowd of high-tech companies.
10. Rao always wears a brown shirt when he goes to town.
11. Americans use ounces and pounds to weigh things.
12. My son astounded the talent scout with his singing.

♫ **Intonation:** Repeat the following phrases, some of which are American idioms. Emphasize the accented syllable for rhythm and interest.

dówntówn	tower of Lóndon	I dóubt it.
brown ców	powdered snów	cóffee grounds
a cold shówer	hourly wáges	raised éyebrows
an ounce of prevéntion	a pound of cúre	on the hóur

[ɔɪ] ► Lesson 31

Sentence: The empl<u>oy</u>ee <u>oi</u>led the iron fittings.

Spelling Combinations for the sound [ɔɪ]

oy as in **employee** **oi** as in **oil**

Production: Start with the jaw open and the lips slightly rounded, as if you were going to say [ɔ]. As you produce sound, drop your jaw slightly, lift your tongue forward and draw the corners of your mouth back.

Most non-native speakers of English do not find this sound hard to produce. There are no significant problems.

Words at Work:

avoid	deploy
point	employ
invoice	enjoy
coil	toy
joint	annoy
boycott	soy
appointment	destroy
embroil	poignant
cloying	recoil
coin	poison
poise	toilet
choice	soil

Practice Sentences for the sound [ɔɪ]

1. Roy appointed several managers to look at the choices.
2. The soy ink spoiled because it was left out and uncovered.
3. If you don't voice your choice, you can't complain later.
4. The convoy of toy boats sailed in Joy's bathtub.
5. Use transparent foils for the new-employee orientation.
6. The boys who changed the oil in my car annoyed me.
7. My employer served oysters at our quarterly meeting.
8. Troy avoids carrying too many coins in his pocket.
9. The mechanic pointed to the coils as the source of the problem.
10. Joyce always boils her food to destroy bacteria.
11. Floyd's group will deploy the workaround next week.

Review Sentences for all diphthongs

1. When I shouted "Fire!" the employees crowded toward the exit sign.
2. I surround myself with bright lights when I'm reading about islands.
3. Hai grounded the wires and attached them with pliers.
4. This alloy has just the right hardness for our coins.
5. I'll buy ninety-five devices if the price is right.
6. I'm just the right height to hide in tight places.
7. Saudi Arabia exports high-grade oil.
8. The angry, oily-skinned pig avoided the joyless butcher.
9. Deployment to our out-of-town customers occurs on Friday.

▣ Idea for a Conversation: an enjoyable day off from work

How might you spend a day off? Talk briefly about your plans for an upcoming holiday or weekend.

►◄ Dialogue

The Company Cafeteria

Mike: How's it going? I don't see you often now that you're at the other site.

Inez: [ɑɪnɛz] I can't complain. I'm getting overtime hours and liking it.

Mike: Let's find a table before the crowd arrives.

[They sit at a table.]

Inez: How about you? Are you enjoying your new job?

Mike: Yes, I enjoy finance. Sometimes it's annoying, however, because people growl about budget items.

Inez: In my department we try to help managers with their authorized accounts. But we're always way behind.

Mike: There's no idle time around our department, either.

Inez: In July I'm going to take a vacation to the British Isles.

Mike: Wonderful. Will you also visit Ireland? I want to take my boys there one day.

Inez: Why don't you take some time off soon? Air prices are not high.

Mike: It's not an ideal time for our family to travel.

Inez: Maybe next year. Wow! I see they're serving free ice cream. Let's get in line for some right now.

Please request your free download of the audio reading of this book.

Simply write to:
downloads@jolindaosborne.com
and put this word in the subject line:

diction

You will receive a reply with easy instructions
on how to download the MP3 audio.

Chapter Eleven
More Communication Skills For Success at Work

- Tips for Speaking on the Phone
- Managing Nervousness
- The Pronunciation of American States and Capitals
- International Phonetic Alphabet List of Symbols
- Index of Difficult Sounds – Arranged by First Language
- Record of Troublesome Words

You may find that coworkers and customers don't always understand you when you speak on the telephone or as part of a teleconference meeting. Your voice must carry all your meaning because listeners do not have eye and facial cues or body gestures to help them understand you. Furthermore, listeners can't "read your lips" in order to interpret your accent. **Thus, clear speech is critical.**

Here are some **tips** for better communication on the phone. Before your meeting begins, take a moment to remind yourself of the following:

- ✓ **Speak directly into the phone or microphone**. Keep your mouth at a consistent distance from the phone/microphone so that your voice doesn't vary in loudness or intensity.
- ✓ Make an extra effort to **enunciate the ending consonant sounds of words,** especially [t, d, f, v, k, g, l, r].
- ✓ **Pronounce the *s* and *ed* endings in order to clarify time/numbers.**
- ✓ **Avoid contractions that might be misunderstood**. Use ***cannot*** rather than can't, and ***do not*** rather than don't.
- ✓ **Avoid idiomatic expressions** that might be not be understood by an international mix of people at your meeting.
- ✓ **Remind yourself of your particular speech and pronunciation issues** [rapid speech, mispronunciation of certain sounds, soft voice, etc.] so that you can make an extra effort to speak clearly in the meeting.
- ✓ When the listener says, "What?" or "Say that again," do not simply repeat what you said without first considering:
    - o *Which words might I rephrase?*
    - o *Was I speaking too quickly?*
    - o *Is my voice too soft? Did I swallow sounds or syllables?*

Tips for Speaking on the Phone [continued]

- ✓ **Slow down!** Give the listener time to get used to your accent, as well as comprehend the information and ideas you are conveying.

- ✓ **If people have difficulty understanding or writing down your name, consider spelling it out.** Following is a variation of the system used in the military.

Say: **"My name is ___________________. I'll spell it."**
"A as in Abel, B as in Boy,….." and so on.

Use this phrasing. Don't just begin to spell. Alert the listener to exactly what you plan to do.

- ➢ Take time to spell your name. Your name is important – to you and to the person with whom you're establishing a working relationship.

Here's the spelling list. Modify it with other words if they are easier for you to say. But remember, you must use simple words that are easily recognizable to the listener and that will leave no doubt as to the spelling of your name.

***Remember to use the pattern: [letter] __ as in [key word] ______**

A as in Abel
B as in Boy
C as in California
D as in Delta
E as in Easy
F as in Four
G as in Go
H as in Happy
I as in Ice Cream
J as in John
K as in King
L as in Lion
M as in Money
N as in Nancy
O as in Open
P as in Paper
Q as in Quick
R as in Roger
S as in Sam
T as in Texas
U as in University
V as in Victory
W as in Water
X as in X-Ray
Y as in Yes
Z as in Zebra

■ **Practice**:

My name is ____________________. I'll spell it.
______ as in __________
______ as in __________
etc.

My company is called __________. It's spelled:
______ as in __________
______ as in __________
etc.

I'm located in __________________. I'll spell that.
______ as in __________
______ as in __________
etc.

Managing Nervousness

Everyone has experienced nervousness when making a presentation. Even senior managers will admit that they are nervous before giving an important talk. Their success – and yours – comes from learning how to control your nervousness so that it doesn't undermine your confidence and the content of your presentation.

Nervousness is shown in many ways, both physical and mental. Here is a list of symptoms people may experience when they're nervous. Luckily, most people don't suffer from all of them at once!!!

dry mouth	rapid breathing	racing heart
perspiration	trembling hands	shaky voice
upset stomach	at a loss for words	use of fillers
flushed face	stuttering	mind goes blank

To make matters worse, employees often find that their accent intensifies!

Following are tips to help you manage nervousness:

- ✓ **Breathe**. No advice is more important that encouraging you to breathe deeply before and during your presentation. [That doesn't mean sighing noticeably into the phone]. Breathe from the diaphragm, as described in **Chapter One**. Increased oxygen to the brain helps you concentrate. Deep breathing slows down your heart and counters a shaky voice. You will feel much stronger as lots of oxygen flows through your body and brain.

- ✓ **Eat lightly** [if at all] before speaking. You want oxygen to go to your brain, not to your stomach in order to digest food.

- ✓ **Drink warm fluids** before/during your presentation. Hot coffee, tea, and hot water with lemon and honey are soothing on the throat. Avoid iced drinks that can constrict the throat, as well as milk, which can produce phlegm.

- ✓ **Drink water** before your talk to hydrate your body. Body hydration will help prevent a dry throat and minimize perspiration. Have water at hand while you are talking. It is perfectly fine to pause to take a sip of water. The pause might even help you recollect your thoughts.

- ✓ **Move your body** while you are presenting. Moving the legs, arms and hands can help dissipate excess nervous energy that has accumulated in your muscles. You might want to take a class or get some coaching in order to incorporate gestures that are natural for your own body and personality.

- ✓ **Pause** if you lose your concentration. Do not use "fillers." Simply stop, take a second to look at your slide or notes to recall what you want to say, and then continue to speak.

- ✓ **Practice difficult words** that you will be using in your presentation. Once you become aware of the words that are consistently difficult for you to pronounce correctly, go over those words so that they come more naturally to you.

- ✓ **Practice aloud.** Silently reading over your slides or notes a few minutes ahead of time is not good enough. You need to ***hear yourself*** speak.

- ✓ **Once you begin, focus on content**. Note your accent issues for later attention, but stay focused on the reason why you're presenting – to deliver content.

American States and their Capitals

Read aloud the 50 states and their capitals. Ask your instructor or a colleague for help with pronunciation and stress.

Montgomery, Alabama
Juneau, Alaska
Phoenix, Arizona
Little Rock, Arkansas
Sacramento, California
Denver, Colorado
Hartford, Connecticut
Dover, Delaware
Tallahassee, Florida
Atlanta, Georgia
Honolulu, Hawaii
Boise, Idaho
Springfield, Illinois
Indianapolis, Indiana
Des Moines, Iowa
Topeka, Kansas
Frankfort, Kentucky
Baton Rouge, Louisiana
Augusta, Maine
Annapolis, Maryland
Boston, Massachusetts
Lansing, Michigan
St. Paul, Minnesota
Jackson, Mississippi
Jefferson City, Missouri
Helena, Montana
Lincoln, Nebraska
Carson City, Nevada
Concord, New Hampshire
Trenton, New Jersey
Santa Fe, New Mexico
Albany, New York
Raleigh, North Carolina
Bismarck, North Dakota
Columbus, Ohio
Oklahoma City, Oklahoma
Salem, Oregon
Harrisburg, Pennsylvania
Providence, Rhode Island
Columbia, South Carolina
Pierre, South Dakota
Nashville, Tennessee
Austin, Texas
Salt Lake City, Utah
Montpelier, Vermont
Richmond, Virginia
Olympia, Washington
Charleston, West Virginia
Madison, Wisconsin
Cheyenne, Wyoming

List other cities, countries, and work-related geographical names that you find difficult to pronounce.

__________ __________ __________ __________ __________
__________ __________ __________ __________ __________
__________ __________ __________ __________ __________
__________ __________ __________ __________ __________

The Phonetic Symbols [Phonemes] of American English

Consonants

Phonetic Symbol	Dictionary Symbol	Key words	Classification
p	p	pen, keep, open	voiceless
b	b	bug, job, habit	voiced
t	t	tap, little, let	voiceless
d	d	dip, middle, lid	voiced
k	k	key, come, pick	voiceless
g	g	gag, give, egg	voiced
f	f	fin, after, phone	voiceless
v	v	vet, serve, five	voiced
θ	th	think, bath	voiceless
ð	th	the, bathe	voiced
s	s	sit, guess, cent	voiceless
z	z	zoo, zip, freeze	voiced
ʃ	sh	shoe, she, wish	voiceless
ʒ	zh	beige, measure	voiced
h	h	how, behind	voiceless
w	w	way, wait, wet	voiced
r	r	run, train, sort	voiced
j	y	yet, annual	voiced
l	l	let, fell, lull	voiced
m	m	man, timer, same	voiced
n	n	no, nine	voiced
ŋ	ng	sing, rang,	voiced
tʃ	ch	chip, watch	voiceless
dʒ	j	judge, edge	voiced

Vowels

Phonetic Symbol	Dictionary Symbol	Key words	Classification
i	ē	be, easy, key	high front tense vowel
ɪ	ĭ	bit, in, tip	high front lax vowel
e	ā	say, plate, eight	mid-front tense vowel
ɛ	ĕ	set, end, red	mid-front lax vowel
æ	a	act, pass	low front tense vowel
ɑ	ä	talk, hot, car	low back lax vowel
ɔ	ô	awful, often	mid-back lax vowel
o	o	go, open, also	mid-back tense vowel
ʊ	oo	book, put, would	high back lax vowel
u	oo	too, moon, true	high back tense vowel
ʌ	u	up, uncle	mid-central vowel
ə	ə	agenda, ago	mid-central vowel
ɝ	ʉr	early, urge	mid-central vowel
ɚ	ər	father, driver	mid-central vowel
ɑɪ	i	five, I, eye	diphthong
ɑʊ	ou	out, how	diphthong
ɔɪ	oi	joy, coin	diphthong

Troublesome English Sounds
Indexed by First Language

Find your first language for guidance on potentially difficult English consonants and vowels sounds. If your first language is not listed, find the language that is closest to your own. The pronunciation difficulties will likely be very similar. Then go to the lessons, review the instruction on sound production, and also listen to the audio version of this book.

ARABIC

- **Consonants:** [p, b, g, f, v, ð, θ, tʃ, ŋ, dʒ, ʒ]
- **Vowels:** [ɪ, ɛ, e, ə, æ, o, ɑ, ʌ]

CHINESE / TAIWANESE

- **Consonants:** [p, b, f, v, ð, θ, n, l, ŋ, r, s, z]
- **Vowels:** [ɪ, ɛ, e, ə, æ, ʌ]

EASTERN EUROPE [CROATIAN, POLISH, SERBIAN, UKRAINIAN]

- **Consonants:** [v, w, θ, ð, ŋ, h]
- **Vowels:** [ɪ, æ, ɑ, ʊ, u, ə, ɛ, ʌ, ɪɚ,]

FARSI

- **Consonants:** [v, w, ð, θ, ŋ]
- **Vowels:** [i, ɪ, ɛ, ɑ, ə, ʌ, ʊ]

FINNISH

- **Consonants:** [p, b, k, g, θ, ð, ʃ, tʃ, ʒ]
- **Vowels:** [ɪ, ɑ, ə, ʌ, ɪɚ]

FRENCH

- **Consonants:** [ð, θ, h, ŋ, tʃ, dʒ]
- **Vowels:** [i, ɑ, ʊ, ə, ʌ, ɑʊ]

GERMAN

- **Consonants:** [b, d, v, w, θ, ð, tʃ, dʒ, j]
- **Vowels:** [æ, ɑ, ʊ, ə, ɪɚ, ɑʊ]

HEBREW

- **Consonants:** [θ, ð, v, w, z, ʃ, j]
- **Vowels:** [i, ɪ, æ, ɛ, ʊ, ə, ɑʊ]

HINDI

- **Consonants:** [v, w, p, t, θ, ð, dʒ]
- **Vowels:** [ɪ, ɛ, e, ə, æ, o, ɑ, ʌ]

ITALIAN

- **Consonants:** [g, θ, ð, r, ŋ, tʃ, dʒ]
- **Vowels:** [ɪ, æ, ɑ, o, ʊ, u]

JAPANESE

- **Consonants:** [r, l, θ, ð, s, ʃ, ŋ]
- **Vowels:** [ɪ, ɛ, ə, ʌ, æ, ʊ,]

KOREAN

- **Consonants:** [p, b, r, l, s, z, tʃ, dʒ, j]
- **Vowels:** [ɪ, æ, ɛ, o]

PORTUGUESE

- **Consonants:** [b, v, θ, ð, ŋ, tʃ, dʒ]
- **Vowels:** [ɪ, æ, ɛ, ʌ, ʊ, u, ɝ,]

RUSSIAN

- **Consonants:** [p, b, t, v, w, θ, ŋ, h]
- **Vowels:** [ɪ, æ, ɑ, ɔ, o, ɝ]

SCANDINAVIAN [DANISH, NORWEGIAN, SWEDISH]

- **Consonants:** [v, w, θ, ð, tʃ, dʒ, s]
- **Vowels:** [æ, ɑ, ɔ, o, ʊ, u, ɝ]

SOUTHEAST ASIAN [JAVANESE, MALAY, FILIPINO/TAGALOG]

- **Consonants:** [p, f, v, b, θ, ð, s, z]
- **Vowels:** [ɪ, ɛ, ɑ, o, u]

SPANISH

- **Consonants:** [b, v, θ, ð, ŋ, j, tʃ, dʒ]
- **Vowels:** [ɪ, ɛ, æ, ɑ, o, ʊ, u, ɪɚ]

SWAHILI

- **Consonants:** [θ, ð, ʃ, k, g, tʃ, dʒ]
- **Vowels:** [ɪ, ɛ, ɑ, o, ʊ, u, ɝ]

TAMIL

- **Consonants:** [g, v, w, θ, ð, n, ŋ, s, ʃ, tʃ, dʒ]
- **Vowels:** [ɪ, ɛ, æ, ə, ʌ, ɑ, o]

TURKISH

- **Consonants:** [p, b, v, θ, ð, ŋ, s, tʃ, dʒ]
- **Vowels:** [ɪ, ɛ, ʌ, ɑ, ʊ, u]

URDU

- **Consonants:** [v, w, p, t, θ, ð, dʒ]
- **Vowels:** [ɪ, ɛ, e, ə, æ, o, ɑ, ʌ]

VIETNAMESE AND THAI

- **Consonants:** [p, t, d, g, f, v, θ, ð, s, ʃ, r, l, ŋ, tʃ, dʒ]
- **Vowels:** [ɪ, ɛ, æ, ɑ, o, ʊ, u, ɪɚ]

Record of Your Difficult Work-Related Words

Coworkers	Customers	Products
______	______	______
______	______	______
______	______	______
______	______	______
______	______	______
______	______	______
______	______	______
______	______	______
______	______	______
______	______	______
______	______	______
______	______	______
______	______	______
______	______	______
______	______	______
______	______	______
______	______	______
______	______	______
______	______	______
______	______	______
______	______	______
______	______	______
______	______	______
______	______	______
______	______	______
______	______	______
______	______	______
______	______	______
______	______	______

Additional Notes

CPSIA information can be obtained at www.ICGtesting.com
Printed in the USA
LVOW032156130212
268563LV00001B/9/P

9 781461 136835